Do You Love Me?

Experiencing and Extending Tremendous Love

Aaron Taylor

Renown Publishing
www.renownpublishing.com

Do You Love Me? / Aaron Taylor
ISBN-13: 978-1-952602-66-5

First and foremost, this book and all of my messages are only possible because of the life, breath, and ability given to me by our glorious Creator and Savior, and His Holy Spirit. Moreover, I hope that all I convey is based solely on the wisdom of God's Word and sound doctrine.

God's influences being a priority, He has influenced this book through my current and past friendships, all of my relationships, the books I have read up to this point, the messages that have impacted me, my travels, and the many other experiences God has given me. I am extremely thankful for the blessings and the life He has given me.

The purpose of this particular book was one that completely changed my life and purpose. I view the people in my life much differently than I ever did before. The truths of this book are simply a revelation of the power of love found in God's Word. I spent many years thinking I was loving God the way He loved me. Today, I view God's love for me, the way I love Him, and my love toward others much differently than I did previously. I am very thankful for this journey. I acknowledge that it has come with failures that have helped me grow, sometimes at the expense of others. Thank you to all who have helped me along the way.

I would like to acknowledge all who have called me pastor through my many years of ministry. I am especially thankful to those who allowed me time to grow and find the power of God's grace and mercy. It has brought me to a place where His love can shine through the trials of my life, our lives together, and this world in which we live.

And I dedicate this book to my wife, Kristy, who has been one of the greatest examples of God's unconditional love toward me. From the day we were married, your support and unquestioned love for me have been empowering.

I also dedicate this book to my late parents, Robert and Joyce Taylor, who showed Jesus by the way they loved each other. My father consistently challenged me to look deeper into God's Word, to find the truth of His Word that consistently reveals itself to those who read it daily. My parents taught and patterned an Ephesians 4 life until it became a part of our family life. It wasn't until they had passed on into glory that I realized the impact they had on me and my future. They lived a humble life without regrets. Thank you for your determination to leave all and follow after Jesus, to teach His Word in truth and without compromise.

I also want to dedicate this book to my children, my grandchildren, and those yet to come. I want the best for you, and I know Jesus is what is best for us all. When we receive His love, we all know how to truly love. I love you all and hope for God's best for your life now and in the years to come.

A special thanks to everyone who faithfully supports our ministry in dedicated service, in prayer, and financially. Your support makes this venture possible, as well as our various messages, sermons, outreaches, discipleship efforts, and gospel-sharing events. Thank you so much!

Lastly, thanks to all those who have helped contribute to this book, including those who have reviewed the book. My book review team was amazing!

CONTENTS

Can I Love Like Jesus? 3

When All Is Stripped Away 9

This Changes Everything 27

Understanding the Love Triangle 41

What Do I Stand to Gain? 53

The Fruitful Love Tree 65

Marriage: An Example of Love 77

God Is Love—Are You? 93

Resembling Our Father 107

When Love Fails 123

Forgiveness 137

What Seeds Are You Planting? 151

How to Wreck a Church with Love 163

How Could a Loving God…? 173

Agape Transforms 179

Notes 183

About the Author 185

About Renown Publishing 187

Can I Love Like Jesus?

So when they had eaten breakfast, Jesus said to Simon Pe-
ter, "Simon, son of Jonah, do you love Me more than these?"
He said to Him, "Yes, Lord; You know that I love You."
—John 21:15

I have lived my life feeling like I knew what it meant
to love like Jesus loved. To give like Jesus gave. Yet, do
I really? When I was preparing a message about an exchange between Jesus and Peter, a message I had preached
many times before, the Lord began to unfold some very
simple, but life-changing, things to me—things about His
Word, about His life, and about mine. It caused me to ask
myself some questions: Do I really love Jesus? Do I really
love Him the way He loves me? Am I even capable of that
kind of love? Do I even have the capacity or ability to love
Him?

If God's love is truly *agape* (unconditional), what does
that mean for me? *Agape* is a Greek word for love,[1] and it
is the God kind of unconditional love—which we will

explore more throughout this book.

When these questions and promptings began filling my mind, God stirred a challenge in my heart. He directed me to discover the way Jesus portrayed love because that reveals how I am able and expected to love. If God is love, then Jesus is the epitome or manifestation of that love. This led me to dig much deeper than I had ever dug concerning a subject I thought I already understood fully.

We are going to dig deep together and make the deep and difficult things of God simple and livable. The revelation I share in this book has changed my entire outlook on loving God and loving others, even after over thirty years of full-time ministry. Maybe most importantly, it has opened an incredible expanse of understanding God's love for me and my ability to share it with the world.

I have shared this message all over the world because it has transformed my life immensely. Every time I give this message, I ask two foundational questions. These simple but thought-provoking questions create the premise for grasping this message fully.

The first question I ask is: "How many people here feel like they unconditionally (agape) love God?" When I ask this question, most hands confidently rise in the room. There are the usual few who don't raise their hands—the non-committal and those who are reluctant to answer anything. I guess some feel like they don't love God, and they also don't raise their hands. But the majority commit to this kind of unconditional love toward God.

The second question is: "Do you love Him the way He loves you?" At this point, a few people reconsider their answer, but most raise their hands confidently again.

Realize, I am not trying to get anyone to not love God, but to understand and answer correctly the same question that Jesus asked Peter—"Do you love Me?"

After these two questions, I make this statement: "We understand that agape is to love like God loves. The true agape is found in Jesus and how He loved. He is truly the definition of love." At this point, most nod their heads in affirmation, feeling confident in their unconditional love for Jesus.

I ask those questions again, expounding on the meanings of the words—which will be supported and defined later in this book. I think we get stuck on the idea of loving God unconditionally; however, Jesus portrayed His agape in a much more life-defining manner.

Next, I challenge their assertion with these questions:

- "Did you love God first?" I ask this because agape loves first, as defined by Christ.

- "Have you loved God when He personally rejected you?" This question reveals that agape is demonstrated in the face of utter rejection.

- "Have you loved God when He left you? Or when He spit on you, mocked you, or mistreated you?" That is the perfect agape love Christ displayed with His life, rejection, and death.

- "Did you love Jesus when He had nothing to give you, expecting absolutely nothing in return?" He has always had so much to offer me, and my expectations of Him are often very high because His promises to me are so great!

The answer (especially to the first three statements) is always the same: "God didn't do those things to me."

In answer to the fourth question, we have many expectations of God, and we trust in His promises. So, for us to say we love God expecting nothing in return would be disingenuous.

After asking some of these pointed questions, I believe everyone starts to understand what the discourse between Jesus and Peter in John 21 was truly all about. The meaning is so different than I thought, and even preached it to be, for years. We have been told and believed that Peter—out of the shame of his denials—could not fully answer correctly when asked if he loved Jesus. However, I don't think that's the full picture or the whole story. In this book, we will take a new look at what it actually means to love like Jesus loves, because I believe Peter who knew the culture and language wanted to answer Jesus correctly but didn't feel like he could.

I think we are often found *wanting* to know how to love Jesus, but unsure if we have the capacity or ability to truly love like He loves us. Together, we are going to explore unconditional love revealed through the nature of Christ Jesus in a way often missed by the most well-meaning and genuine Bible teachers, theologians, and truly born-again Christians.

We will discover how we can truly answer yes to the question Jesus asked Peter: *"Do you love Me?"* We can not only say yes to that question, but we can also tap into a love that will affect every relationship we have and make eternal the purpose of our love.

Additionally, we'll define and access the supernatural circle of love. This will provide for us a well or reservoir with an unending supply—and will remove from our friends and family our impossible demands to meet our needs and expectations that only the work on the cross can really meet.

We can find a place of contentment when we receive this love God has given us by His Spirit. We can be empowered to give it to others when we are walking in the refreshing supply of God's love.

After each chapter, workbook sections will provide questions and action steps that will posture you to allow God's great love to transform your life.

I hope that when you finish this study, you will walk away with a heart that is able and willing to daily explore the love of God in rewarding ways—one that is ready to declare your love for your Lord and to receive His love in return. One in which you can enjoy the unending fully satisfying, unconditional love of God. It's a tall order, but one Jesus died for, and through His Spirit makes possible in and through you daily.

Often, I read a book for a few chapters, feel like I get the meaning, and stop reading. I strongly encourage you to read this volume to the very end, because the simple truth you'll learn about grows throughout the book into an expansive and fundamental truth. This won't just open up a few ideas for you; it may show you a new way of walking out your Christian faith.

CHAPTER ONE

When All Is Stripped Away

Love is not something you simply feel or experience, but a journey we are all on. Too often on this journey, we don't entirely grasp the depth of our love for someone until they're absent. In other words, sometimes, we have to lose love to appreciate it fully.

Can you imagine what it was like for the disciples after Jesus was crucified? The man they believed was the Messiah—the man who was supposed to end the Roman oppression, their beloved friend—had been brutally slain. The disciples feared everything they believed in—and all they had hoped for—was lost.

But Peter's grief was so much heavier than some. He had denied he even knew Jesus three times on the night when Jesus was tortured and killed. Fear had gotten the better of Peter and he'd refused to be associated with the Christ (Matthew 26:69–75). And what was worse, Jesus had told him this would happen earlier that evening (Matthew 26:31–35). So, Peter knew his shame was fully known in advance by the very person he betrayed.

Then Jesus rose from the dead. Suddenly, all of His promises made sense. The prophecies of old were fulfilled. Finally, the disciples better understood what it was that Jesus came to earth to do.

But could they forget that just a few days ago they were swallowed in doubt and sorrow? Could Peter push from his mind the memory of denying Jesus? Could he distance himself from the failure he had been when Jesus needed him the most?

When Jesus first revealed Himself to Peter after resurrecting, Peter was fishing. The catch became breakfast Jesus shared with the disciples. During breakfast, this sobering exchange occurred—one that is so reminiscent of when Jesus first called Peter, recorded in Luke 5:1–11, when He said He would teach them to be fishers of men. Maybe it reminded Peter of when he walked on the water with Jesus. But one thing was certain—when Peter recognized it was Jesus, he dove out of the boat and swam to Him.

So when they had eaten breakfast, Jesus said to Simon Peter, "Simon, son of Jonah, do you love Me more than these?"

He said to Him, "Yes, Lord; You know that I love You."

He said to him, "Feed My lambs."

He said to him again a second time, "Simon, son of Jonah, do you love Me?"

He said to Him, "Yes, Lord; You know that I love You."

He said to him, "Tend My sheep."

He said to him the third time, "Simon, son of Jonah, do you love Me?" Peter was grieved because He said to him the third time, "Do you love Me?"

And he said to Him, "Lord, You know all things; You know that I love You."

Jesus said to him, "Feed My sheep. Most assuredly, I say to you, when you were younger, you girded yourself and walked where you wished; but when you are old, you will stretch out your hands, and another will gird you and carry you where you do not wish." This He spoke, signifying by what death he would glorify God. And when He had spoken this, He said to him, "Follow Me."

—John 21:15–19

Whenever I read this passage from the Gospel of John, I am struck by the intensity of this exchange between Jesus and Peter.

Here at this meal, the disciples sat with Jesus. Imagine their deep joy and contentment. Surely God who raised His Son from the dead would do marvelous things through Jesus' followers!

When Jesus turned to Peter and asked if he loved Him, of course Peter replied, "Yes, Lord."

But there's more to that question than we first see. Matthew 22:37 shows us just how much Jesus asks of us. As we progress through this book, you will discover how much weightier it is—yet doable.

When asked what the greatest commandment is, Jesus references Deuteronomy 6:5: "You shall love the LORD your God with all your heart, with all your soul, and with all your mind."

Well, now, that's asking rather a lot, isn't it, Lord?

We're to use all our hearts, souls, and minds to love God? I certainly can't say I measure up to that. If that's how God expects us to love Him, does anyone have a chance of being successful? Maybe the Apostle Paul or Mother Theresa might, but not me! Can I truly love like that?

Yet, this is how God expects us to love Him. It's how He deserves to be loved. Our reaction to the question, "Do you love Me?" shouldn't be to shrink away, knowing we can't measure up. Or like Peter to say, "I love You, but not like You love me." If you aren't sure what I mean when I say Peter didn't love Jesus the way Jesus loved him, keep reading. The explanation is coming.

If you've been around the church for any amount of time, you know what the word *agape* means—it's one of the many Greek words for love.[2] You've probably heard many a sermon on agape love. Depending on the linguist or philosopher you may listen to or read, you can find many different meanings and definitions of the word translated into English as *love*. Both Greek and Hebrew words used for love have different meanings. Jesus was trying to convey truths in a way the people present at the time would understand deeply, and the writers used the dialects of their days to relay the truth of Jesus to the listeners which ultimately reveals the truth to us today.

You know, the love God calls us to is different from *eros*, which is sensual love or romantic love of a sexual nature.[3] The New Testament, written in Greek, refers to it, but not directly—and usually in the areas of caution (1 Corinthians 7:8–9).

Storge is familial love, referring to the affection or relational, natural love that characterizes the relationship between parents and children. Storge is instinctual and protective, like we have toward our very close friends or close family.

The love God calls us to is not *phileo*, or brotherly love, either.[4] This kind of love is what you see most often. It looks like, "When you're good to me, I will reciprocate and be good back to you."

In truth, phileo is what almost all of our relationships seem to be based on, whether good or bad, positive or negative, short- or long-term. Scratch my back and I will scratch yours. You help me and I will help you. I am good to you, and you be good to me. Our marriages are often built on this format also, but I believe the Lord has so much more for us than that. There is a supernatural fruit that comes from the Lord. This is what Jesus was talking to Peter about, and He is also speaking to us about it.

The love God asks of us is so much more unique.

But I don't just want to get out my dictionary and read you the definition. You see, the word *agape* describes a love that is beyond any dictionary definition. It's true meaning can only be understood by studying it in action— the Jesus kind of action. The Bible says that Jesus is love (1 John 4:7). He is truly the manifestation of the love for all people from the Godhead. Jesus is the revelation of love to us. Love isn't just a word you can define with a single sentence; it is revealed in the person of Jesus Christ.

I have done lots of counseling, and in pre-marriage counseling, I often ask, "What would cause you to divorce?" They usually start by saying nothing would. I then say, "What about infidelity?" "Well, I guess that would and I would be justified." How about abuse?

One day I realized that if infidelity is a just reason for

us to pursue divorce, then whenever I have been unfaithful to God, I have given Him a just reason to divorce me. I am not arguing divorce or even the law concerning divorce. I am saying God has given us a love that can overcome anything and as we receive unconditional love from Him, He expects us to give it to others.

It's easy to love when things are good and easy, but what about when things are not? When everything is stripped away, we get to love like Jesus loves us. When we've made some definite mistakes or failures, we find a love like no other. I have discovered that unconditional love has no conditions of failure. Now *that* is a love worth having. This is God's love toward us. When we don't love Him—when we can't love Him, when we fail at loving Him—He still agapes us. What would happen if we loved like that, not because we feel like it but because He loved us like that?

This realization brought me to tell my wife, "No matter what, I love you." Faithful to me or not, good to me or not, I want to love her like Jesus loves me. Honestly, I am not capable of it without God's help. I can only love like that when I receive and realize that kind of love. She is so faithful and giving, so I honestly have no concerns, but I want to invest the kind of love that causes her to love me all the more. I want to love her the way Jesus has loved me. This will nurture the kind of relationship that will last. This is the kind of relationship we are called to have that covers a multitude of sins and shortcomings.

Jesus Is Love

We throw around the word *love* a lot. We love pizza or we love the color red. We love our pet, our friends, our new car, or our favorite football team. In English, we have one word that we use to cover all kinds of love. No wonder we have a hard time understanding what it means to love God! It's also sometimes hard to understand how God is trying to convey Himself to us.

Agape love isn't the sort of thing you can fully understand by words alone. This is why Jesus lived it for us. Let me give you some advice: the place to start learning about agape is in Jesus. And if you ever get to the point where you think, *"I've got this all figured out,"* you're wrong. The road to agape is truly a journey. Slowly, step by step, God reveals a bit more about what agape truly is. Your eyes will suddenly see a new aspect they couldn't before. Your heart will suddenly be able to love a little better.

As humans, we're accustomed to feeling the God-given need for love. Even if we don't put a voice to it, our hearts cry out, *"Do you love me?"* all the time. It may seem odd to think that Jesus—that God—asks us the same question. He doesn't need love in the same way we do, but He desires our love, nonetheless. God realizes we cannot give His love fully until we learn to receive unconditional agape from Him.

Naturally, the love God gives and expects in return is far above what we are able to receive and give on our own. Our very best examples of love are tainted by our sinful humanity. In order to truly understand how God loves us and how we are to love Him in return, we must examine the living example of love—Jesus Christ.

The truth is, Jesus is love. He is the perfect example of agape love. This is why I am reluctant to lug out my dictionary and give you a bland definition. In reality, Jesus' life on earth is the definition of agape love. To understand it, we must study how Jesus lived and loved when He was on earth.

Let's start with the fact that Jesus came to earth at all. God spent four thousand years letting His people attempt to follow His laws and live rightly with Him. All the while, He was displaying His unconditional love and nature to them. And they failed in enormous ways. Adam and Eve lived in perfect agape with God in the garden of Eden. Within a generation, one of their sons killed the other (Genesis 4). Just a thousand years after the garden, the world was so evil and corrupt that God wiped it out with a flood, saving only a few lives (Genesis 6:1–9:17).

The Israelites were God's chosen people. They were given priests to help them uphold the law, judges to steer them right, and eventually kings because they begged for a human ruler. Look at the lineage of Christ and you'll see Israel's whole sordid history laid out: murder, deceit, adultery. Sin after sin after sin.

All of this sin was against God. Every single one was a betrayal of His love for His people. And what did He do about it? God sent His Son (part of Himself) to earth to be the sacrifice for the sins committed against Him. Why would He do that? Because of agape. He didn't do it for what He would receive, but because He loves (agapes) us.

Imagine someone killed a person whom you love with all your heart. The case goes to trial. During the trial, you step in front of the judge and declare that you forgive the murderer. But more than that, you say you will go to prison in their place. You will pay the price for the atrocity committed against you and your family. It's unthinkable, right?

That is a tiny glimpse of what Jesus did for us. And it was the only way for God to bring His beloved people back into right relationship with Him. That kind of love is unprecedented, unfettered, and unfathomable. It's both bewildering and magnificent in its intensity and power. This is the power of love. *This* is agape.

Love Displayed

You might be familiar with the "Love Chapter" in the Bible, which is 1 Corinthians 13. If you've been to any weddings, you've likely heard it read many times. The love described in this chapter is a nice thought, though not really a standard we successfully hold ourselves to.

When all is stripped away—good, bad, and indifferent—we need to see the priority of love. Let's never allow good works, giftings, or ministry to replace actual agape. Love is God's greatest priority. Love is actually the purpose of good works, our calling, our giftings, our families, and our ministries:

> *Though I speak with the tongues of men and of angels, but have not love, I have become sounding brass or a clanging cymbal. And though I have the gift of prophecy, and understand all mysteries and all knowledge, and though I have all faith, so that I could remove mountains, but have not love, I am nothing. And though I bestow all my goods to*

feed the poor, and though I give my body to be burned, but have not love, it profits me nothing.
—1 Corinthians 13:1–3

This explanation of love is the way Jesus lived. He walked in agape perfectly. To get a better glimpse of this, let's trade out the word *love* for "Jesus." This shows us the qualities and attributes Jesus lived with as He walked out agape. As you read this, ask yourself the question, *"Do I love like this?"*

Jesus suffers long and is kind. *Do I love like this?*
Jesus does not envy. *Do I love like this?*
Jesus does not parade Himself. *Do I love like this?*
Jesus is not puffed up. *Do I love like this?*
Jesus does not behave rudely. *Do I love like this?*
Jesus does not seek His own. *Do I love like this?*
Jesus is not provoked. *Do I love like this?*
Jesus thinks no evil. *Do I love like this?*
Jesus does not rejoice in iniquity but rejoices in the truth. *Do I love like this?*
Jesus bears all things, believes all things, hopes all things, endures all things. *Do I love like this?*
Jesus never ends. Jesus doesn't stop loving! *Do I love like this?*

When we love like Jesus, we really do show agape! Jesus showed us agape is revealed when everything is stripped away and there is nothing to personally gain, and you still choose to give, expecting nothing in return.

Love is the embodiment of who God is toward us, and

we should be the embodiment of who God is toward others.

That is the definition of agape.

Agape in Action

The term *Christian* was coined in the city of Antioch, from an insult the people bestowed on the disciples there (see Acts 11:26). It translates as "little Christ," or "little anointed one," and was meant to belittle Jesus' followers.[56] But, what an honor! To be a version of Christ is the goal of all Christians, isn't it? To start and end with our Christ-like love—there is no better place to be!

Being a Christian boils down to our actions. We are to live in such a way that people around us notice that we are Christ-like (1 Peter 2:12). It isn't all about what we say or the rituals we go through.

Jesus' love is revolutionary. It flies in the face of logic. It stands in stark contrast to even the most "Christian" societies. Jesus touched the untouchable. He made time for the marginalized. He associated with women, with tax collectors, with known pariahs and outcasts. When we love God and others with agape, it confounds the people around us.

Jesus actually hung around the people who would not ever be allowed in the holy place, especially not the holy of holies. Jesus, upon His death, tore the veil between us and Father God in two. He took His presence to the people, and loved and accepted them where they were, where they lived, while also giving them hope for much more. Religion—Christian religion often included—expects people to come to God. Yet Jesus has come to you because He loves you and wants to love through us all.

How do you treat the people around you? Do you love them the way Jesus loves you? You see, when Jesus was asked by the Pharisees which was the greatest commandment, Jesus said loving God was the most important, but then He went on. Matthew 22:39 says, "And the second [command] is like it: 'You shall love your neighbor as yourself.'"

Not only are we to love God with agape, but we are to love each other with agape, too. In fact, loving the people in our lives with agape is a way that we respond to our Heavenly Father with love. Loving others in this manner is made possible by receiving agape from our Heavenly Father. Unless we receive that love (agape) first, we are unable to give that love. We are capable of giving brotherly love (phileo), but true agape comes from God.

The Preeminence of Love

> Love never fails. But whether there are prophecies, they will fail; whether there are tongues, they will cease; whether there is knowledge, it will vanish away. For we know in part and we prophesy in part. But when that which is perfect has come, then that which is in part will be done away.
>
> When I was a child, I spoke as a child, I understood as a child, I thought as a child; but when I became a man, I put away childish things. For now we see in a mirror, dimly, but then face to face. Now I know in part, but then I shall know just as I also am known.

And now abide faith, hope, love, these three; but the greatest of these is love.
—1 Corinthians 13:8–13

I believe verse 13 makes it clear that we cannot even have hope or faith without love. The preeminent thing in every relationship, and in all of life, is love! It's who God is, and it's what matters most. It is the impetus for faith, and it is what gives us hope. Everything that we are and have was birthed out of God's love for His creation. His unconditional love birthed His salvation for us.

When all was stripped away from Jesus, He became a sacrifice to bring eternal life for all humanity. John 3:16 says, "For God so loved the world that He gave His only begotten Son, that whoever believes in Him should not perish but have everlasting life." My paraphrase of this verse is: because He loved us with agape, He gave His love to and for us.

The common love *phileo*, as we discussed earlier, begins and ends with what *we* can get out of it. Agape takes it further and chooses to be good to others even if we get nothing in return. This book will continue to explore this kind of selfless love. My hope is that together we will gain more understanding of what Jesus exemplified so we will be able to answer yes when He asks, "Do you love Me?"

WORKBOOK

Chapter One Questions

Question: In what ways do you think your love for others mirrors Jesus, and in what ways does it not? Do you love more with phileo or with agape love?

_____

_____

_____

_____

_____

_____

_____

_____

_____

_____

_____

Question: Where do you see love in action in the world today? Who in your life models agape love? To whom and in what ways are you demonstrating active, agape love?

_____

_____

_____

_____

_____

_____

_____

_____

_____

_____

Memorize and Personalize: Read 1 Corinthians 13:4–8 and choose a version in which to memorize these great verses. Think about how each of the qualities described in those verses is exemplified by Jesus. Then evaluate how true it is in your own life. Choose one or two of the attributes of love to begin focusing on this week. Ask God to help you to learn to show love like He does.

_____

_____

_____

_____

_____

_____

_____

_____

_____

_____

Further Study: Do a study on the book of Hosea. What insights does this story give into the nature of God's love? Journal your thoughts and questions from your study.

_____

_____

_____

_____

_____

_____

_____

_____

_____

Chapter One Notes

_____

_____

_____

_____

_____

_____

_____

_____

_____

_____

_____

_____

_____

_____

_____

_____

_____

_____

_____

_____

_____

_____

_____

_____

CHAPTER TWO

This Changes Everything

It's easy to love the Apostle Peter. He makes all of us feel like we could be welcomed into God's family because bumbling, enthusiastic, over-eager Peter was. I think Jesus had a special place in His heart for Peter. This is the disciple, after all, who received some really important lessons about the kingdom of heaven, and about agape in particular.

Let me show you what I mean.

The Love Discussion

I quoted this passage in the last chapter, but I want to put it here for you again. This time, though, I'm going to use the Greek words for love (from Chapter One) as they appear in the original text. I think Jesus does something remarkable here.

So when they had eaten breakfast, Jesus said to Simon Peter, "Simon, son of Jonah, do you [agape] Me more than these?"7

[Peter] said to Him, "Yes, Lord; You know that I [phileo] You."8

[Jesus] said to him, "Feed My lambs."

[Jesus] said to him again a second time, "Simon, son of Jonah, do you [agape] Me?"9

[Peter] said to Him, "Yes, Lord; You know that I [phileo] You."10

[Jesus] said to him, "Tend My sheep."

[Jesus] said to him the third time, "Simon, son of Jonah, do you [phileo] Me?" Peter was grieved because He said to him the third time, "Do you [phileo] Me?"11

And [Peter] said to Him, "Lord, You know all things; You know that I [phileo] You."12

—John 21: 15–19

Did you catch that exchange? Remember that this was after Peter denied knowing Jesus three times before His crucifixion. When Peter and Jesus had this conversation from John 21, Jesus had just arisen from the dead. In this conversation, there seems to be some deep understanding between the two of them.

It's easy to miss why Peter couldn't bring himself to say that he loved Jesus with agape.

We modern American Christians are often in the same boat with Peter on this, aren't we? We are willing to be loved by God with agape, but we're only able to love Him with phileo in return. We expect God to love us unconditionally, to forgive our every sin, and to fight furiously on behalf of us. In return, we are really sorry when we sin but make no real change. We'll love our neighbors, friends, and family until it gets too hard or too messy or they don't love us back. We'll sit in our usual pew every single Sunday—except for when we're at the lake or it's too rainy or little Timmy's baseball games get in the way. Or when we don't like the music anymore. Or if we are not recognized for something the way we think we should be. Or if, God forbid, the pastor or leadership doesn't measure up to our standards. We ask for mercy for ourselves and expect judgment for others. On the cross, Jesus called out for mercy for us who crucified Him and sinned against Him.

And then we are shocked when God gives us a reality check and allows some actual suffering in our lives to draw us closer to Him. Someone comes along and asks us to show agape and, like Peter, we say, "I mean, I grew up going to church, but I'm not sure I'm the best person to visit you in prison."

The dilemma here isn't that we don't want to agape God. I believe Peter, more than anything, wanted to answer Jesus with agape but he realized that he couldn't. It may not be for the reasons you think. Could it be that it wasn't because of his failures towards Jesus, but his failure toward others? It could be that he had not received the fullness of God's Spirit to supply him the ability to love like Jesus had loved him. Maybe Jesus understood the words being used here much more than we do. The depths of these words really do matter and could possibly unlock a transformational message in our lives, families, churches, and maybe even the world in which we live. In the very same way, we feel it is impossible to agape God even though we are commanded to. If this is true, is God asking us to do something we cannot do?

> *"Teacher, which is the greatest commandment in the law?"*
>
> *Jesus said to him, '"You shall love the LORD your God with all your heart, with all your soul, and with all your mind.' This is the first and great commandment. And the second is like it: 'You shall love your neighbor as yourself.' On these two commandments hang all the Law and the Prophets."*
>
> **—Matthew 22:36–40**

Like Peter, we are unable to do it. Remember the introduction of this book and the first chapter? If love is defined by who Jesus Christ is, then how can we or Peter agape Jesus? Consider, once again, these questions from the Introduction:

- *Did you love God before He loved you?* The answer is no! He first loved us (1 John 4:19).

- *Have you loved God when He rejected you?* Romans 11:1–12 makes it clear that He hasn't rejected, nor will He ever reject, His people. So no, you have never had the opportunity to love Him in the face of rejection.

- *Have you loved God when He left you?* Hebrews 13:5 makes it clear that God has not and will not leave us or forsake us. It's His nature to agape. So the answer is no! You've never had to love God that way.

- *Did you love Jesus when He had nothing to give you, expecting absolutely nothing in return?* He has always had so much to offer me and my expectations of Him are often very high because His promises to me are so great!

If true agape is to love first, to love when forsaken, and to love expecting nothing in return then Peter knew he could not answer Jesus with the word *agape*. He had to use the word *phileo* because that was the extent of his capacity to love. A reciprocal love. The kind of love that only give to the extent it receives.

The real question remains: How can I agape God, who has loved me before I had the chance to love Him—who has never rejected me and will never forsake me—all the while expecting nothing in return?

All you can do is receive this kind of love.

Once you get this point, it will change your understanding of every Bible verse you read about love. They will take on a completely different meaning for you. Did Jesus ask us to do something impossible when He asked us to agape Him (Matthew 22:37)? This command in Matthew comes from the Ten Commandments that were given to Moses for humanity.

Jesus asked Peter a simple question on the surface, "Do you agape Me?" Peter was well aware that he had already failed Jesus. Yet Jesus kept pouring out His love on Peter even in the midst of that failure. This isn't the main reason for Peters response—"phileo." I believe Peter knew he was incapable of that kind of love, a love that would later become a fruit of the indwelling Spirit. It was a love that he could not possess for Christ, because Jesus had already shown such perfect agape towards him. Peter said, "I phileo you. I *respond* to your love." Because Peter knew that in the context of their relationship, Jesus was the one *giving* love and received nothing in return. And Peter was the one responding to what he received from Jesus. But Jesus showed Peter many ways to love Him with agape.

How Do We Change Our Phileo to Agape?

Jesus has told us exactly how to love with agape. He said it in His discussion with Peter in John 21. Did you spot it? It's in His responses to Peter: "Feed My lambs… Tend My sheep… Feed My sheep." Peter was called to show agape to the people around him. *This is how he shows agape to God.*

Peter couldn't love God first in the face of rejection, or love God when God abandoned him, because God will never do those things. However, Peter can love his neighbor that way. And in this passage, Jesus was revealing that is the way we are able to show our agape for Him.

It's so simple, isn't it? And yet, it's not an easy task. I mean, surely pouring my heart out through worship shows God my agape, right? Giving generously to the building fund shows God my agape, right? Memorizing dozens of Bible verses shows God my agape, right?

That isn't what Jesus told Peter. When Peter said he loved Jesus with phileo, the response wasn't, "Worship more." Nope. Jesus instructed Peter to care for other people who could do nothing in return.

Wow! Jesus was saying very personally to Peter what God has been attempting to communicate to humanity throughout all time! He was once again saying, "This is My commandment, that you love one another as I have loved you" (John 15:12).

It's a "receive from God in order to give to others" message. Not a "give to get from people" message. Jesus freely gives us agape so we can agape others. But how does that give us the answer to the question, "Peter do you love Me?'

The best scripture to shed light on what Peter was realizing is found in Matthew 25:37–40:

> *"Then the righteous will answer Him, saying, 'Lord, when did we see You hungry and feed You, or thirsty and give You drink? When did we see You a stranger and take You in, or naked and clothe You? Or when did we see You sick, or in prison, and come to You?' And the King will answer and say to them, 'Assuredly, I say to you, inasmuch as you did it to one of the least of these My brethren, you did it to Me.'"*

We will cover this more in subsequent chapters but *wow!* Did you see that? Jesus was saying "I love you with agape which enables you to love others with agape—loving them first, loving them when the love is rejected, expecting nothing in return—and in doing so, you are loving me." *Whatever* you do to the least of these, you are doing unto God. This is what I like to call the Love Triangle, which we will discuss this in the next chapter.

When we look at this passage through the lens of agape, it is very clear what Jesus was saying: "Unless we love others with agape, we don't love God." Loving God in return with phileo won't cut it. In fact, without agape love for the people around us, we're no better than the Pharisees who thought that following rules would get them what they wanted.

Let me clarify this even further. We don't love others with agape love to work our way into heaven; we don't love others to earn God's approval. Loving others is the *fruit* of a heart that has been transformed by God's agape love! When you experience God's love for you, it will naturally spill over onto others. Have you tasted and seen that the Lord is good (Psalm 34:8)? If you have, it will be evident in the way you treat those around you.

Agape Changes Everything

For those Christians who understand this and start pursuing God's agape, everything changes. Suddenly, God's discipline isn't a punishment we should be ashamed of. Rather, it's a loving act from the One who wants our best. It's like when my wife points out that I need a mint. I don't grumble and act upset that she noticed my flaw. I appreciate that she doesn't want me to embarrass myself around others.

We understand that our Father is gently shaping us to be more mature. As we grow and learn, He trusts us with more responsibility. Thankfully, He never dumps everything on us all at one time. We get to learn, instead, one lesson at a time. We deal with one sin issue at a time. We master one discipline at a time.

It's tempting for us to look at more mature Christians and get discouraged. "Look at how he or she's handling this hardship. I could never do that" we may say. We listen as people in our small group or Bible study discuss what they're learning, and we feel so far behind.

Listen, I'm not going to hand my car keys to my ten-year-old. Not a chance! She simply isn't ready to handle all the thought processes that need to happen. Her legs haven't grown long enough to reach the pedals. In six years, she'll be ready (kind of ready), but she has some growing to do.

And as we learn these lessons, we turn and apply them to the people around us. That is how we agape God. We show the same grace to our families that God showed us. We fail, we repent, we ask forgiveness, and we learn from it. We forgive and restore like we have been forgiven and restored. We humbly accept that God loved us with agape first and out of our appreciation, we agape others. When someone rejects agape, I'm not devastated because I'm just passing on God's agape. Being willing to give it freely even when rejected is what makes it agape! This doesn't come from us; it comes from God. So go to Him! Receive agape from His endless supply and then turn and share it with others.

WORKBOOK

Chapter Two Questions

Question: Would you describe your love for Jesus as *phileo* or *agape* love? What actions or attitudes back up your assessment? How can I truly agape God without it simply becoming works-based? How is receiving God's love different from earning it?

_____

_____

_____

_____

_____

_____

_____

_____

_____

_____

Memorize and Personalize: Memorize and study Matthew 25:31–46. In what specific ways can you minister to practical and spiritual needs such as those described in this chapter?

_____

_____

_____

_____

_____

_____

_____

_____

Further Study: Read a biography or memoir about the life of a missionary or aid worker who devoted their life to "the least of these." How did God's love motivate them and how did they show their own love for God through feeding His sheep and tending His lambs? The story of five American missionaries who gave their lives to reach the Huaorani (Waodani) people of Ecuador definitely touched my life. It was not just the story of those who gave their lives but also of their families who carried on after them. (You can find this story in the book _Through Gates of Splendor_ by Elisabeth Elliot and the movie _End of the Spear._)

_____

_____

Chapter Two Notes

_____

_____

_____

_____

_____

_____

_____

_____

_____

_____

_____

_____

_____

_____

_____

_____

_____

_____

_____

_____

_____

_____

_____

CHAPTER THREE

Understanding the Love Triangle

Every TV drama seems to include a good love triangle. Those love triangles usually have one person as the focus, with two other people vying for that person's affection.

Has God put us in that kind of love triangle? Where He's competing with everyone else in the world for our love? No, that isn't the kind of love triangle I'm talking about.

First of all, our so-called love for our common man is often phileo love, focused on manipulating them for what we can get for ourselves. The love triangle God has invited us into is not like the love triangles so common on TV dramas or in movies. Genuine unconditional love has no need for competition. In fact, when we receive perfect love from God, we can love those around us more completely.

A Supernatural Gift

Some will be offended at this statement, but the reality is—not everyone can love with true agape. In fact, the closest we come to agape in our human abilities is a Greek term called *storge*.[13] Storge is the love a parent has for their child. But even that intense, instinctual love from parents for their children doesn't reach the height and depth of God's agape.

Listen to the words of 1 John 4: "Beloved, let us love one another, for love is of God; and everyone who loves is born of God and knows God." This verse is not saying that everyone who loves with human love is born of the Spirit of God, or a born-again Christian.

There are many people who love others with various types of love who are obviously not born of the Spirit of God. What this verse says is, "everyone who *agapes* (the love that comes from the Spirit of God) is born of God and knows (is in relationship with) God."

God manifested His love toward us. God's love is like a thirty-six-inch pipe connected to a half-inch pipe. As long as the small pipe stays connected to the larger pipe, it will have more than enough supply. We can always increase our capacity to love because the source of the love will always be enough. We often try and make other people love us to get the love we need, but it is never enough. They end up feeling drained and we feel neglected and unsatisfied. Mother, father, husband, wife, children, family, or friends cannot fill us with enough love the way God does. This leaves us feeling neglected and unable to love others the way we need to because we don't receive the love we need to be truly fulfilled. It's like we are trying to siphon what we need from relationships, instead of freely pouring into them the love God is freely pouring into us.

> *Beloved, let us love one another, for love is of God; and everyone who loves is born of God and knows God. He who does not love does not know God, for God is love. In this the love of God was manifested toward us, that God has sent His only begotten Son into the world, that we might live through Him. In this is love, not that we loved God, but that He loved us and sent His Son to be the propitiation for our sins. Beloved, if God so loved us, we also ought to love one another.*
>
> **—1 John 4:7-11**

Verse 11 at the end of this passage gives us more proof of what Jesus was revealing to Peter in John 21. If God so agapes us, we also ought to agape others. God isn't in competition with other people, but He wants you to have the love you need to love them correctly and unconditionally. We receive from Him so we can give to others. That may seem simple, but we are talking about love that gives expecting nothing in return. Loving them not as a work of righteousness but from an abundance of the love of God we receive from a right and overflowing relationship with Christ.

Understanding Something We Can't Understand?

In Ephesians 3:19, the Word tells us that we can know something beyond human understanding. The "thing" we can know is the supernatural love of God! As we walk in faith, believing the love of God is poured out more and more, what was impossible becomes possible. We may have been empty, but now we can be filled with the love of God.

> *For this reason I bow my knees to the Father of our Lord Jesus Christ, from whom the whole family in heaven and earth is named, that He would grant you, according to the riches of His glory, to be strengthened with might through His Spirit in the inner man, that Christ may dwell in your hearts through faith; that you, being rooted and grounded in love, may be able to comprehend with all the saints what is the width and length and depth and height—to know the love of Christ which passes knowledge; that you may be filled with all the fullness of God.*
>
> *Now to Him who is able to do exceedingly abundantly above all that we ask or think, according to the power that works in us, to Him be glory in the church by Christ Jesus to all generations, forever and ever. Amen.*
> *—Ephesians 3:14–21*

The following diagram may best explain what Holy Scripture is showing us over and over and over again:

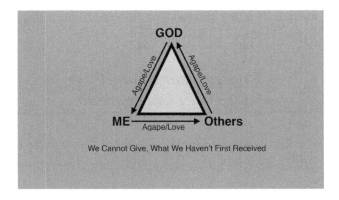

This is what Jesus was saying to Peter and what we will see over and over in Scripture. God pours out His unconditional love for us by His Holy Spirit within us and through us, without expecting anything in return. When we receive it, we then have the capacity to walk in His love. When we give it to others, truly expecting nothing in return, our love is not only for others but also, ultimately, unto the Lord.

"Peter, do you agape me? Then go agape someone else like I agaped you, and when you have done it, then you have fully shown agape to me."

We may try to love others out of works, and maybe our own personal grit and determination. The problem is, we will grow tired and empty. We will feel used and even abused. When we are receiving what we need from the Lord, we are receiving from a well that never will run dry.

That's part of what Jesus was revealing to the woman at the well in John 4:1–26. She had been looking for love in all the wrong places. In fact, looking to find love in marriage after marriage and man after man—yet she was still unfulfilled. She was coming to a well that would leave her thirsty. Jesus said, "There is a time coming and now is that time," speaking of the coming Holy Spirit, "when the well will dwell in your heart and not in a mountain. This water will be a spring of life that will spring up in life to us all" (paraphrased).

When we begin to walk in agape, we begin to walk from a place of revelation and understanding that reveals Christ in ways that religion and works cannot reveal. Yet it also draws us to a place where we long for more of

Christ and not less. To do more of His kingdom work, not less. To love more like Jesus, not less.

God's Love in Action Will Bring Revelation

In the counseling portion of my work, I often find that many people want to know the will of the Lord for their lives or their purpose. They need direction. When we read this in 1 Corinthians 2:9–12, we see that God is longing to reveal His will, His giftings, and even the depths of God to those who agape. He will freely bring the revelation of things not known or easily discerned by the flesh and will reveal Scripture to those who agape. As you go out and give God's agape to others, He will bring greater understanding of who He is and His will to you. That makes me want to love more and more. To love others and in doing so, to manifest my love for God.

> But as it is written: "Eye has not seen, nor ear heard, nor have entered into the heart of man the things which God has prepared for those who love Him."
>
> But God has revealed them to us through His Spirit. For the Spirit searches all things, yes, the deep things of God. For what man knows the things of a man except the spirit of the man which is in him? Even so no one knows the things of God except the Spirit of God. Now we have received, not the spirit of the world, but the Spirit who is from God, that we might know the things that have been freely given to us by God.
>
> **—1 Corinthians 2:9–12**

This love opens up so much more than a works-based law. It is the law of the love of God given to many through the Holy Spirit who dwells in each one of us. You want to operate in the gifting of God? Love like God loves. You want God's wisdom? Love like God loves. You want to understand prophecy and Scripture? Start by finding people who can give you nothing in return and actively love them. In this triangle of love, we will find the understanding we need in trying times. The opportunities to love are all around you. God will provide you with everything you need as you give love in tangible ways.

There are a couple reasons I considered calling it the circle of love instead of the triangle of love. The first reason is because we can easily expand the circle of love we have. The second is because a circle has no beginning and no end, showing the agape of God never fails or comes to an end. The second reason is also the reason I choose to stick with the triangle concept of explanation. True agape is a gift. It comes as a gift and comes from our God to us by His Spirit.

Chapter Three Questions

Question: What is the "love triangle" God is inviting you into? How does it differ from the love common in this world?

_____

_____

_____

_____

_____

_____

_____

_____

_____

_____

_____

Question: Who are the people you find yourself turning to most often to fill you with love? Where are the places you go? What are the habits you turn to? Think of all the times you have gone to someone/something other than God seeking to be filled? What was the result?

_____

_____

_____

_____

_____

_____

_____

_____

_____

_____

_____

_____

Memorize and Personalize: Memorize Ephesians 3:14–21. Have you experienced the width, length, depth, and height of the love of Christ? Have you allowed God to fill you will all the fullness of God? Take a moment to invite God to fill you with His love.

_____

_____

_____

_____

_____

_____

_____

_____

_____

_____

_____

_____

Further Study: Study the woman at the well in John 4:1–26 in greater depth. What does her story reveal about God's love?

_____

_____

_____

_____

_____

_____

_____

_____

_____

Chapter Three Notes

CHAPTER FOUR

What Do I Stand to Gain?

What will I get if I give to others? If I agape, what do I stand to gain? The hard truth is that if you give agape hoping to gain, then it isn't agape anymore.

This will irritate some who have lived their lives giving to get; it will also concern those who are afraid of being taken advantage of. Please read on to understand fully. God knows our hearts and wants to bless His children and does. His blessing comes when we live out the kingdom principles of God. We live in His kingdom spiritually and it releases the kingdom abundance into our natural lives. Sometimes this abundance comes in what money can buy and sometimes it comes in much more than money can ever buy. We receive from Jesus, the sower, good seed in our lives. I will try to cover a little more of this basic principle later in the book. What do we do when we receive the seed or life-giving supply from Him? We do what Jesus told Peter in John 21:15–17, "Feed My lambs... Tend My sheep... Feed My sheep." We receive agape from

Him to give, expecting nothing from the lambs or sheep.

"What do I get then?" This is the attitude of the world and its systems. I am sad to say it has crept into many churches. They minister to the tithe payers, or potential tithe payers, because that's how it works. It's an understandable and natural system, one I have been swept away in, but it's not God's way. It's easy to get caught up in this system. This thinking will lead you to despise the poor and needy. This is not agape. Do you agape Jesus? Then give to the hurting, broken, the least, and you will show agape to Jesus. Don't give so you have a place in church, in an organization, or even to gain a place in someone's life. Give because He has given to you first. Like those praying in Matthew 6, love not to gain someone's attention.

In Luke 6:20, Jesus began with the amazing Sermon on the Mount also recorded in Matthew 5 and Luke 6. This is a passage that is so profoundly descriptive of the heart of Jesus concerning agape. Please don't skip over the beatitudes quickly, because they also show God's heart about agape and about entering into life in His kingdom. We ask, "What do we get from agape?" Well, read this:

Then He lifted up His eyes toward His disciples, and said:

"Blessed are you poor, for yours is the kingdom of God. Blessed are you who hunger now, for you shall be filled. Blessed are you who weep now, for you shall laugh. Blessed are you when men hate you, and when they exclude you, and revile you, and cast out your name as evil, for the Son of Man's sake. Rejoice in that day and leap for joy! For indeed your reward is great in heaven, for in like manner their fathers did to the prophets."

—Luke 6:20–23

"But I say to you who hear: Love your enemies, do good to those who hate you, bless those who curse you, and pray for those who spitefully use you. To him who strikes you on the one cheek, offer the other also. And from him who takes away your cloak, do not withhold your tunic either. Give to everyone who asks of you. And from him who takes away your goods do not ask them back. And just as you want men to do to you, you also do to them likewise.

"But if you love those who love you, what credit is that to you? For even sinners love those who love them. And if you do good to those who do good to you, what credit is that to you? For even sinners do the same. And if you lend to those from whom you hope to receive back, what credit is that to you? For even sinners lend to sinners to receive as much back. But love your enemies, do good, and lend, hoping for nothing in return; and your reward will be great, and you will be sons of the Most High. For He is kind to the unthankful and evil. Therefore be merciful, just as your Father also is merciful."

—Luke 6:27–36

Verses 32–36 speaks volumes. It's easy to love those who love you. Even the world can do that. It's not overly spiritual to love the people who care and sacrifice for you. It's not saying you shouldn't, but it is saying that if you want to show agape to Jesus then you have to love extraordinarily.

Love like Jesus—love first. Don't wait for them to come to you. Love your enemies, love those who spitefully use you. Love expecting nothing in return. When given every right to not love, go ahead and love. Love like Jesus loved you and keeps loving you so you can keep loving them.

Many years ago, I got a hold of some memorabilia from certain sports teams, including my favorite team.

I knew some people who had once been my friends yet had decided to turn against me and say all kinds of evil about me. I knew those friends would enjoy this gift—but I also knew they wouldn't receive it well from me. Plus, I didn't want to break up the complete set of memorabilia I had collected. God began to work on my heart, though.

I wrestled with God for days. I asked God, "What about me? They don't deserve to be happy. Why should I bless them when they have only tried to hurt me and speak evil of me?" I decided to bless them through a mutual friend.

God also spoke to my heart, "I don't ever want them to know you did this." One has passed away, and I am sure the other is unlikely to read this book, so I will continue. I thought, "How will this restore the relationship? I will just be out the things I want and enjoy with nothing to show for it in return!" Ultimately, I knew what I had to do. Early in the morning, around 2 a.m., I snuck to their houses and laid these gifts at their doors. I've honestly never heard another word about it.

You may think that was the end of the story. Not really Many years later, I had the opportunity to be in each of their homes and both of them had the gifts proudly displayed. When I saw them, I wanted to say, "Wow, nice. I wish I had those," but I chose not to say a word. The reason was because from the night I covertly gave them those gifts, something changed in me toward them. I no longer held any bitterness. I was free.

Later we did get the opportunity to reconcile but to this day, I haven't said a word because it wasn't about them. It was about God wanting to do a work in me. God needed to do a work of forgiveness in my heart. I needed to freely love them for their benefit alone, not expecting anything in return—not even a thank you. I was blessing what was, at the time, my enemy.

Honestly, it has begun a series of many covert operations. I find ways to bless people without others knowing who or where it came from. Not always, because sometimes it's good that they know where it came from and that it comes in the name of the Lord.

This event was so life changing because it caused me to give expecting nothing in return. I was loving Jesus. It was the best thing I could ever do. I never fail to find blessing when I am obedient to Jesus. He is a great rewarder.

This Is a Message of Risk Management

Luke chapter 6 is all connected. Jesus went on to talk about not judging others, about giving and God's blessing, and about fruits of blessing and the words of life or death. Then Jesus told the story of two men—one who built his house on the rock, and one on the sand. These stories were all told in the context of the beatitudes and loving your enemies with true, unconditional agape. Such love is defined by the life and words of Jesus. Let's read the rest, until we get to the story about building on the rock in Luke 6:37–49 (emphasis mine):

> *"Judge not, and you shall not be judged. Condemn not, and you shall not be condemned. Forgive, and you will be forgiven. Give, and it will be given to you: good measure, pressed down, shaken together, and running over will be*

put into your bosom. For with the same measure that you use, it will be measured back to you."

And He spoke a parable to them: "Can the blind lead the blind? Will they not both fall into the ditch? A disciple is not above his teacher, but everyone who is perfectly trained will be like his teacher. And why do you look at the speck in your brother's eye, but do not perceive the plank in your own eye? Or how can you say to your brother, 'Brother, let me remove the speck that is in your eye,' when you yourself do not see the plank that is in your own eye? Hypocrite! First remove the plank from your own eye, and then you will see clearly to remove the speck that is in your brother's eye.

"For a good tree does not bear bad fruit, nor does a bad tree bear good fruit. For every tree is known by its own fruit. For men do not gather figs from thorns, nor do they gather grapes from a bramble bush. A good man out of the good treasure of his heart brings forth good; and an evil man out of the evil treasure of his heart brings forth evil. For out of the abundance of the heart his mouth speaks.

*"But why do you call Me 'Lord, Lord,' and not do the things which I say? Whoever comes to Me, and hears My sayings and does them, **I will show you whom he is like**:*

"He is like a man building a house, who dug deep and laid the foundation on the rock. And when the flood arose, the stream beat vehemently against that house, and could not shake it, for it was founded on the rock. But he who heard and did nothing is like a man who built a house on the earth without a foundation, against which the stream beat vehemently; and immediately it fell. And the ruin of that house was great."

"I will show you whom he is like"—rarely do we put this scripture in the correct context of scripture. Jesus was about to talk about the meaning of this scripture. He was speaking of His love and forgiveness, in and through us, being the firm foundation on which we stand in obedience or actively live out agape, as God intended.

In this parable, Jesus was directly referring to the context of loving—especially loving strangers and your enemies. Here, He said it's about risk management. When you build on the words and actions of Christ to love, you have a sure foundation. Things are solid and will stand all the winds and waves, the storms of life. He didn't say they wouldn't come because they surely come. In fact, He promises we will experience tribulations, but we will overcome when we hear the words of the Lord and do them.

The benefits of living in true agape will become evident. We receive agape from God, we give agape to others expecting nothing from them, and through that we show agape to Jesus, so that we can say, "Yes, Jesus, we do agape You!"

Chapter Four Questions

Question: Do you have the tendency to love others only if you know you will receive something in return? Can you love others expecting nothing in return through your own strength?

_____

_____

_____

_____

_____

_____

_____

_____

_____

_____

Question: Who is someone difficult for you to love? What is something you can do for them—expecting nothing in return—to show them God's love? Ask God to fill your heart with His love for them.

_____

_____

_____

_____

_____

_____

_____

_____

_____

_____

_____

Memorize and Personalize: Memorize Luke 6:32–36. Is this kind of love visible in your life? Why or why not?

_____

_____

_____

_____

_____

_____

_____

_____

_____

_____

_____

_____

Further Study: Read Luke 6:35–45. How does this portion of Luke 6 tie back to the Jesus' theme of loving expecting nothing in return?

_____

_____

_____

_____

_____

_____

_____

_____

_____

_____

_____

Chapter Four Notes

CHAPTER FIVE

The Fruitful Love Tree

Let's make sure we start this amazing chapter in full understanding that all the fruits of the Spirit—as well as the gifts of the Spirit—hinge on love. There is nothing before love. There is nothing that stands alone or apart from love. The fruit of the Spirit gives us the metaphor of things that grow from a vine or a tree. This is simply put: love, as well as all the fruit of the Spirit, should be produced or grown from the innerworkings of our relationship with Christ.

> *But the fruit of the Spirit is love, joy, peace, longsuffering, kindness, goodness, faithfulness, gentleness, self-control. Against such there is no law.*
> **—Galatians 5:22–23**

So, when Paul calls the effects of life in the Holy Spirit *fruit*, it's not surprising. Trees, bushes, and vines produce the fruit their DNA dictates. As we begin to trade our sinful nature for God's holy nature, it's only natural that the fruit we produce changes, too.

These characteristics line up exactly with agape, don't they? If someone was loving (agape), joyful, peaceful, patient, kind, good, faithful, gentle, and under control, he or she would be showing agape.

What is particularly interesting about this list is that they are described as fruit which comes from the Holy Spirit. Fruit grows over time and requires careful tending. If we pull away from the Holy Spirit, we cannot grow these characteristics in a healthy way.

One more thing I want to point out is that fruit, unlike flowers, is only beneficial when it is taken from the tree and consumed. A flower can be beautiful as long as it stays where it is. Fruit, however, is designed to be eaten. Similarly, the fruit of the Spirit is only beneficial when it is put into practice. Until it's given away, it's worthless or, at most, unattainable beauty from a distance.

The Vine, the Branches, and the Fruit

In John 15, Jesus told an amazing parable about fruit. This shows us another very descriptive metaphor of the triangle of love. Jesus is the Vine, we are the branches, and our fruit is not for our consumption but for others to eat of without worry because we received that fruit from the vine. Let's start with the pruning process found in John 15:1–17:

> "I am the true vine, and My Father is the vinedresser. Every branch in Me that does not bear fruit He takes away; and

every branch that bears fruit He prunes, that it may bear more fruit. You are already clean because of the word which I have spoken to you. Abide in Me, and I in you. As the branch cannot bear fruit of itself, unless it abides in the vine, neither can you, unless you abide in Me.

"I am the vine, you are the branches. He who abides in Me, and I in him, bears much fruit; for without Me you can do nothing. If anyone does not abide in Me, he is cast out as a branch and is withered; and they gather them and throw them into the fire, and they are burned. If you abide in Me, and My words abide in you, you will ask what you desire, and it shall be done for you. By this My Father is glorified, that you bear much fruit; so you will be My disciples.

"As the Father loved Me, I also have loved you; abide in My love. If you keep My commandments, you will abide in My love, just as I have kept My Father's commandments and abide in His love.

"These things I have spoken to you, that My joy may remain in you, and that your joy may be full. This is My commandment, that you love one another as I have loved you. Greater love has no one than this, than to lay down one's life for his friends. You are My friends if you do whatever I command you. No longer do I call you servants, for a servant does not know what his master is doing; but I have called you friends, for all things that I heard from My Father I have made known to you. You did not choose Me, but I chose you and appointed you that you should go and bear fruit, and that your fruit should remain, that whatever you ask the Father in My name He may give you. These things I command you, that you love one another."

Pruning

Oftentimes, plants have branches which need to be cut off because the branch dies but keeps taking needed nutrients. Other branches might become diseased and require removal before the healthy branches are infected. Sadly, some branches might need to be removed because they have stopped receiving life from the vine.

As we consider moving toward loving people, especially the unlovely, it's tempting to pull the "I'm too busy" card. This idea of pruning is vital. If we do not deal with diseased areas of our life, then God will have to. If we don't remain connected to the vine, we will suffer loss, be completely separated, wither and even experience death. We must examine and evaluate every part of our lives. Are there diseased things you go to regularly? Prune them. Is your life so cluttered that you can't make room for agape? Prune the nonessential things back. Are there things in your past that do you no good, yet you continue to cling to them? Prune them. Or, maybe I should say, let the Father take them without your struggle to keep them. They clutter your life and take your strength. When my father, Robert Taylor, taught me to prune trees, he showed me what was not beneficial. He would call them sucker limbs because they took the sap, strength, and life from the tree, reducing their productivity.

Some people take this to mean that anyone who is not producing good fruit should be removed from our lives. Please remember you are a branch, and the Father (or husbandman) removes the branches, not us. The Father will trim away the things that sap our strength. Allow Him to do that and remember your production of fruit isn't about you and others. It's about you and Him.

You have to start with remaining healthy yourself before you can truly be a help to others. It is vital you remain in God's Word and continue to receive life from His Spirit. You have to be healthy to help others. You must abide in the vine. That's really the main point for us to take away in this passage about receiving to give love, or agape.

Abiding

Let's not ignore the other important part of this: we only grow the fruit of the Spirit when we are connected to the Spirit. A seed in a packet next to a pot of soil is never going to grow. Only going into the soil and staying in the soil will allow that seed, in time, to become a plant. We need to abide in God.

If we stop abiding, we are not receiving from the Spirit who gives us this fruit. Our works are also affected, and we stop worshiping, growing, giving, learning, and encouraging. Perhaps this happens slowly, but it does happen. Without God there to keep us going, our love grows cold. Over time, we stop producing fruit. A tree that doesn't produce fruit is often on its way to death.

That's a heavy thought, isn't it? Either our spirits are connected to God and growing, or they are disconnected and dying. There's no in-between, no middle of the road. If I stop speaking with my amazing wife, our relationship will be in bad shape very quickly. With no communication or connection, our relationship will degrade.

By the way, my wife Kristy is amazing. No, she didn't make me write that, but I do know what's good for me. No communication, and we will grow apart within a very short time. The statement of our marriage is to "grow closer together every day or we will grow daily farther apart." Many people wake up after twenty years of marriage and wonder who they are married to. That doesn't happen overnight, but day after day growing apart. We must keep our communication in order to stay on the same page with our children, our finances, and our marriage.

We aren't ever going to be able to agape others if we are disconnected from God. If we aren't connected to Him, we'll pour ourselves out and have nothing refilling us. Without the Holy Spirit, agape is impossible. We must prioritize spending time with the Father. He is our source of agape. Without Him we can show love but not the kind of agape that only comes from a connection with Jesus.

Fruitful

Let's not ignore the fruit. It doesn't come from us; it comes from the source. It comes from the life giver. We once again see the example of the triangle of love. The love of God flows through the vine (Jesus) to the branches (us) and produces fruit for others. What does that fruit do to benefit the tree? Nothing. The fruit is meant to be eaten to bring life to others or to fall to the ground to produce more trees. What it doesn't do is benefit the branch. Why do we keep expecting it to? Why do we show love expecting our love to be reciprocated and then become disappointed and often upset when it isn't?

We love others and then have expectations because we want the benefits to come back to us. This example of the vine and the branches shows we must receive what we need for our life and what we need to produce fruit from *the vine*. It all comes from the vine. We freely receive and we are meant to freely give. This is one of the best pictures of unconditional love and faith. We love and show the fruit of the Spirit freely. We do this in faith that God will provide what we need.

Freely through the vine, we receive the fruit, and freely it is given to bless others. Our faith is to bless others. Our joy will bless others and our love will bless others just like Jesus blesses us. This is not a life of isolation. As a branch I produce and freely offer my fruit. I receive fruit—whether it's good or bad—from the people around me. Eat good fruit and you will live well. Give good fruit because you are connected to Christ Jesus!

Fruit of Faith

Faith is what makes agape so different. Not faith in others but faith in our Source. Faith that God will supply our needs according to the unending, richness of His love towards us. Remember His supply is much greater than our need and even our ability to give it away. The vine (or tree trunk) is much larger and can supply all the branches with what they need, and can also supply enough for all the fruit that grows on the branches.

This is why we need to lower our expectations of the people we are showing love to and just freely, unconditionally show them love. The Bible says that "while we were still sinners, Christ died for us" (Romans 5:8). He gave love to us when we didn't deserve it.

Some not understanding would say, "But He expects us to serve Him or He will send us to hell." The truth is that we are already sentenced to death and ultimately hell, but He has made a way for us to live eternally with Him. God doesn't have to "send" us to a place for which we already are destined. It is because of our sin and separation from God that we already deserve that fate.

By contrast, because of His love for us, God made a much better way for us. Because Jesus loves us, He has made a place for us in His kingdom. He gives us full access to who He is and what He has. That begins now, in this life, by the Spirit, and continues into eternity.

God is an unconditional giver. He gives to us and, through us, to others. The parable of the vine and branches is an amazing way to see agape delivered to us through the vine, and then to others by our fruit. Remember, we don't eat the fruit we produce; we receive from the vine and produce fruit meant to feed others.

What does your fruit look like? Does your fruit look and taste like Jesus to others? We are known by our fruit. When people eat of our fruit, they should taste the Lord— tasting and seeing that the Lord is good. Phileo love isn't inherently bad, but it doesn't taste like Jesus, because it seeks what it can get in return. Agape tastes like Jesus, because He laid down His life to bring you eternal life. Be fruitful and multiply the love of God to others.

WORKBOOK

Chapter Five Questions

Question: What are the fruits of the Spirit? How are the fruits of the Spirit connected to agape? What are some of the diseased, nonessential, or hindering "branches" in your life that need to be pruned? How will you remove these things from your life to make room for growth in agape love?

_____

_____

_____

_____

_____

_____

_____

_____

_____

Question: How is the parable of the vine and the branches reflective of the type of love triangle God calls us to in relationship with Him? Is the fruit you produce in your life for you or others?

_____

_____

_____

_____

_____

_____

_____

_____

_____

_____

Memorize and Personalize: Memorize Galatians 5:22–25. Spend some time in prayer asking God to produce this fruit in your life. Journal about what it means for Christ to produce fruit in your life. How have you experienced the strength and fruit of abiding? How have you experienced the disconnect and barrenness of trying to live the Christian life in your own strength?

_____

_____

_____

_____

_____

_____

_____

_____

_____

_____

_____

Further Study: Find a book or article on gardening. Read about the pruning process and why it helps plants thrive. What analogies can you draw from the natural pruning process that apply to the spiritual one?

_____

_____

_____

_____

_____

_____

_____

_____

_____

_____

Chapter Five Notes

CHAPTER SIX

Marriage: An Example of Love

Throughout the Bible, marriage is used as a metaphor for how God loves His people. I find that very interesting, because it would seem more natural to me for the metaphor to be a parent and a child. It is that, too, but I believe the greatest metaphor is marriage.

I think I can understand why God chooses this metaphor, at least in part. In most instances, we don't choose our children. A child is born to us and that's the one we get. But in marriage, there is a choice involved. It takes place between two sinful adults. Grace and forgiveness must be a part of creating a strong marriage—you have to keep choosing each other every day.

In fact, some theologians argue that marriage was created in order to demonstrate God's love for us, not the other way around. Ephesians 5:22–33 tells husbands and wives how to treat one another by pointing to how Jesus loves His church. Jesus will never leave the church, and the church will never want any other love than Christ's. In the same way, a husband isn't supposed to leave his wife, and a wife is never to want any other love than her husband's. Sometimes we fail in our earthly marriages. Sometimes we fail as husbands, but our Jesus never fails.

If we as men truly loved our wife with agape—like Jesus loves the church—there would be little to no divorce in the church. Rarely does a wife come to me angry saying, "Pastor this husband of mine is way too loving. He seems to always show me love first. I am his primary concern. Sometimes I am having a bad day and I take things out on him. It's so frustrating because he doesn't get upset and never says mean things. He just gives and gives like he has some unending supply of love from God. He's always so joyful, at peace, longsuffering, and shows me kindness. He's so good to me and the kids, and I know he is faithful to me. It's like he lives and walks in the Spirit. I just want rid of this man!"

Okay, that has never been said to me by anyone, or *about me,* quite honestly. Yet if either a man or a woman would have enough faith and trust in God to live from what God has put into them, it would revolutionize their life.

Ephesians 5:25 says, "Husbands [agape]...." Ladies, if your husband isn't doing this, then *you* can give it a whirl. Not because they deserve it. Instead, do it because you're doing it as unto the Lord, the One who does deserve it. Remember He was talking about us submitting to Him as our husband because He loves us like this. He was also asking us to do the same to our spouse.

Husbands, love your wives, just as Christ also loved the church and gave Himself for her, that He might sanctify and cleanse her with the washing of water by the word, that He might present her to Himself a glorious church, not having spot or wrinkle or any such thing, but that she should be holy and without blemish. So husbands ought to love their own wives as their own bodies; he who loves his wife loves himself. For no one ever hated his own flesh, but nourishes and cherishes it, just as the Lord does the church. For we are members of His body, of His flesh and of His bones. "For this reason a man shall leave his father and mother and be joined to his wife, and the two shall become one flesh." This is a great mystery, but I speak concerning Christ and the church. Nevertheless let each one of you in particular so love his own wife as himself, and let the wife see that she respects her husband.

—Ephesians 5:25–33

When I was younger in ministry, I had lots of ideas about marriage that were, quite frankly, immature and foolish. I used to think that if my wife cheated on me, I would leave her in an instant. There was a very short list of things, but a list none the less, that were "deal breakers" for me.

After I realized that Jesus' love for His people is the example I was to follow in my marriage, things shifted dramatically in my heart. No longer would I make up situations in which I justified leaving my wife. Jesus will never leave His people; therefore, I will never leave my wife.

As I mentioned earlier, I actually went to my wife and said, "I'm not going to threaten to leave you under any circumstances, including infidelity." I never had any reason to expect it, but I needed to say it for another reason. I told her, "I don't care what you do, I'm going to love you. I will always be married to you."

You see, I want my wife to love me because she chooses to do so freely, not because she's afraid of me or worried I might get angry and stomp away. Yes, I want my wife to be faithful to me. But I want her to be faithful because of her love for me and most of all, my love for her. A marriage is not built on the fear of rejection or failure but on the security of acceptance. I didn't want my wife to fear my rejection or to live under a threat of repercussions if she failed. That is not what God does for me. I have been unfaithful to the Lord in my heart, thoughts, and even spent a time of rejecting Him openly as a young man, yet His agape has never (yes, *never*) failed me. He has always forgiven me.

Some may say that's going too far and that I would have the grounds for divorce in the instance of infidelity. Yes, I agree and that may be completely true. The problem is, I have found myself the unfaithful bride in my covenant with Jesus. Instead of divorcing me, He chose to love me and forgive me.

I am not trying to argue divorce or remarriage. What I am saying is I can't hold my wife in a place of threat that Jesus hasn't held me to. If my wife was unfaithful to me and I used the rights I have for divorce or even the threat of it against her, how is that right? I have been unfaithful to Jesus (we have all been the unfaithful bride who He is making pure). Is it right to hold my wife to a standard I have already failed at?

Remember agape is not about what you receive from someone. It is about giving to them. We receive from the Lord.

Some may find this hard to swallow and if you, like me, have failed at this very thing, then don't miss this very important part of agape. Husbands are supposed to love their wife as Christ loved the church and gave Himself up for her. He gave himself up for an unfaithful bride, not a perfected one! Husbands are asked to do the very same thing. Since He has loved me in my unfaithfulness, can I also do this for others as I walk in His mercy and grace? Can you?

Jesus' agape love welcomes me back when I sin against Him time and again. Though I worship other gods, Jesus doesn't stop loving me. He patiently waits for me with open arms. I might have to deal with some serious consequences of my sin, but God continues to love me.

My parents (for clarification: my adoptive parents who raised me, Robert and Joyce Taylor) had a very strong marriage by the time I came around. They had a rough first twenty years of marriage, but God revolutionized their lives. They began working on their relationship and understanding what it meant to "appreciate each other more and expect less." They spent much of my life teaching and speaking on marriage whenever the doors opened up. This was the lifelong theme of their marriage: "Expect less and appreciate more." Lower your unreasonable expectations and appreciate others as you do life with people. This theme is a powerful way to live agape for others.

Love Is Not Flashy

Though I speak with the tongues of men and of angels, but have not love, I have become sounding brass or a clanging cymbal. And though I have the gift of prophecy, and understand all mysteries and all knowledge, and though I have all faith, so that I could remove mountains, but have not love, I am nothing.

—1 Corinthians 13:1–2

I remember one Christmas play I was in as a child. I wanted to play the big drum or the drum set, but instead, Bill Clark got that role while I got the role of playing the finger chimes. I still remember it forty plus years later. The song went: "I found it (I chimed my finger chimes) and you can find it to." That was the extent of my purpose in the Christmas play. Yes, you may have guessed it, my timing was off, and I messed up the whole song.

I sometimes wonder if we are afraid to stand before the holy God of the universe and offer up our small ability to love Him. God is so big and has done so much for us. Surely, what I have to offer Him isn't worth giving.

Look at those verses above from 1 Corinthians 13. It doesn't matter if we have big, flashy gifts or enormous amounts of wisdom or such big faith that we can move mountains. Those things are fine, but they don't compare to love.

I take great comfort from considering who it was that Jesus chose for His disciples. There were better teachers, more noble and many with greater abilities, but instead He chose average, every day, blue-collar fisherman. And

Matthew was a hated tax collector, for goodness' sake!

God looks at us and sees something we don't. If you love Him as best you can—which means to agape the ones who can do nothing for you—that love is an offering that pleases the Holy God of the Universe more than dramatic prophecies and showy acts of faith.

Think about the people in your life who have shown you great love. If you've been through a difficult time of great suffering, it's often the little moments that mean the most. Someone who brought a meal or sat with you or asked a thoughtful question can show more love than someone doing something big and showy.

Relationships Are Key

When you're on your deathbed, love takes priority. As a pastor, I've been called to my share of deathbeds. I can assure you—no one ever lies there wishing he could see his expensive car one last time. Instead, words of love are shared, and old hurts are forgiven and forgotten.

Recently, I spent thirty-two days in the hospital, twenty-two of them in ICU. Seven times I went to sleep very unsure if I would live through the night. The doctors were unable to reassure me or my wife. Everything that really matters became very evident. Love shared is what is eternal. I found an amazing peace in the love God has for me and all I wanted to do was share that love.

In the end, relationships are what matter most. Our relationships with others and our relationship with God are the only eternal things we can have in this life. There will be no standing before God's judgment throne and explaining that we gave a lot of money to the poor, attended church weekly, worshiped Him for many hours, and tried to be good. The only thing that will matter is whether or not we accepted Jesus' sacrifice on the cross for the forgiveness of our sins and then walked in right relationship with Him. We walked in the flow of His Spirit.

Matthew 25:31–46 tells us, though, that our loving treatment of the people around us will demonstrate whether or not we loved Him. What we did for those who came into our lives counts as though we were doing those things for Jesus Himself. In other words, the relationships we have on earth with other people have eternal significance.

It's impossible to truly love others without a relationship. Being nice isn't the same as loving others. In order to love, we must know and be known. That's not an easy thing to do. There are people in my life whom I love without any struggle or drama. Others, though, are much more demanding. Does that excuse me from loving them? No way!

Agape is not based on how good you are to me. It's based on how good God already has been to me. My love for you isn't because of what you do; it's based on what God has already done. It isn't an equal give-and-take relationship. Rather, it's recognizing that God has given us far more than we could ever deserve or pay back. From there, we go ahead and pass on the little bit we are able to do as humans.

Jesus died willingly for the sins I committed against Him. Yes, I can serve the homeless population in my city.

God has forgiven every sin I have ever committed rather than blot me out as I deserve. Of course, I can give up my Saturday afternoon to sit with a neighbor who is going through a crisis. I can care for someone the way I want to be treated. Is that so hard? I can care for someone the way Jesus has cared and is caring for me.

I love serving in third-world countries. I show up, not to get, but simply to give, love, and bless the people there, because Jesus has already blessed me. When I've been abroad, many times I have been given an offering. I didn't understand their currency, but I could buy a meal with it. The love that oozed from that was unbelievable. I have even been given a (live) chicken many times! I've always felt the heart behind the gift; the people have such a heart even with very little to give. Their love is so evident. They may have very little monetarily, but their love is beyond explanation. I often feel way more blessed, even though I came to be a blessing.

Hold Tight

I know a lot of men who struggle with the concept of being the Bride of Christ. In our overly macho culture, we've learned to work hard to prove we are not feminine at all. If this is you, spend some time asking God to help humble your heart so you can understand fully how He loves you and how you are to love Him in return.

In the book of Hosea, God shows us that His love for us is like that of a husband with an unfaithful wife. Though we leave Him and betray Him, He buys us back and restores us to the place of honor at his side.

Are you familiar with the book of Hosea? Hosea was a minor prophet whom God commanded to marry a prostitute. So, Hosea did just that. He married Gomer who was a harlot (Hosea 1:2). Together, they had children and God used this little family as an example of how He would treat the people of Israel.

We know that Gomer left Hosea and went off with another man into adultery, because in chapter 3, God commanded Hosea to go and bring his wife back. In fact, Hosea says that he had to buy his wife back from the man she was with.

Other than feeling sorry for Hosea, this book evokes a great deal of emotion and reveals so much about God's love for us. Not only does He come to us in our sin, but He also chooses us when we betray Him. God doesn't throw up His hands and say, "Well, you cheated on me. You're off sinning and worshiping other gods. That's it for us."

No! He comes for us and brings us back to Him, paying dearly so that we can be together. What depths of love He must have! Now, that is agape! And we find it in the Old Covenant.

In Hosea 2:19–20, God promised Israel, "I will betroth you to Me forever; yes, I will betroth you to Me in righteousness and justice, in lovingkindness and mercy; I will betroth you to Me in faithfulness, and you shall know the LORD."

In contrast to Gomer, Song of Solomon 3 describes what our response to God and His love *should* be. Here, a woman awakes to find that the man she loves is missing. She runs out at night to find him. When they are reunited in verse 4, she says: "Scarcely had I passed by them, when I found the one I love. I held him and would not let him go."

Our love for Jesus should cause us to leave everything behind to run after Him and then hold tight as one who has found a precious treasure (Matthew 13:44). The disciples gave up their homes and families to follow Jesus during His life. After His death and resurrection, ten of the remaining eleven disciples were killed for their faith, yet none renounced Him.[14]

How do we love God? We prioritize that relationship, valuing it above all else. We choose to spend time reading God's Word, praying, listening to the Holy Spirit, and loving the people around us with great joy. We need to remember that the greatest example we have of our relationship to Jesus is marriage. We are asked to submit to an amazing husband who loves us, continues to forgive and make sacrifices for us. We are simply asked to love others the way He loves us.

Chapter Six Questions

Question: How has Christ demonstrated His love for you in spite of your failings, unfaithfulness, apathy, and unbelief? Who are some people in your life who have shown you unconditional love? How? Was their love demonstrated through something big and showy or quiet kindness and faithfulness? Explain.

_____

_____

_____

_____

_____

_____

_____

_____

_____

Question: What is your mission statement for showing love in your life? What about in your marriage (whether you're married now or might be in the future)?

_____

_____

_____

_____

_____

_____

_____

_____

_____

Memorize and Personalize: How, specifically, you can show agape this week?

_____

_____

_____

_____

_____

_____

_____

_____

_____

Further Study: Study the lives of the apostles from the Bible and church history. What evidence do you see that these were ordinary men when Jesus found them? How did His love transform them? How did they prioritize their relationship with Christ above all else and prove their love for Him?

_____

_____

_____

_____

_____

_____

_____

_____

_____

_____

Chapter Six Notes

CHAPTER SEVEN

God Is Love—Are You?

My wife and I love our kids. Because we love them, we work to make sure their needs are met, that they are supported when they face hardships, and know we love them. We discipline our children so they can become the best adults possible. Sometimes they don't fully understand the reasons for that discipline, just like we don't often understand God's correction of us. We work to teach them how to be honest, patient, and considerate of others.

However, if our kids grow up and never once extend these lessons to anyone else, we're going to be disappointed. We've poured out our love on them! If they turn out to be selfish and rude, they never learned how to love. They received plenty of it, but something's missing. I would begin to wonder if my children ever really knew their mother and me if they believe it's acceptable to be completely self-absorbed—that's not how we raised them.

I'm sure you see the picture I'm painting. Our

Heavenly Father has poured out agape on us, yet many of us are too apathetic to pass that on. We don't understand the cost Jesus paid or the reality of eternal life and eternal death. We feel no sense of urgency to share the truth of the cross with nonbelievers. Instead, our eyes are entirely centered on our own temporary lives.

To live this way completely denies the example He set. In the story of the sheep and the goats (Matthew 25:31–46), it's clear that the "sheep" know their Father and are like Him. The "goats," on the other hand, are absolutely clueless!

The Sheep's Example

Let's assume I've convinced you that we show God agape by loving other people with agape. Maybe you're eager to move forward. The next logical question is: What does that look like exactly? How do I love others through the course of my everyday life?

Those are fair questions. Jesus was perfect all the time. It's daunting to try to emulate His example when there are so many gray areas in life. It's always wrong to steal from my boss or lie or damage his car when I'm angry. Those things are easy to spot. But, how do I show my boss agape on a daily basis? Fortunately, there are two passages in the New Testament in particular that give us a clear picture of what we're called to be.

The first passage I've already mentioned: The Sheep and the Goats. When Jesus described what the sheep had done, He was spelling out for us precisely how we are to live. Let's look at this one more time:

Then the King will say to those on His right hand, "Come, you blessed of My Father, inherit the kingdom prepared for you from the foundation of the world: for I was hungry and you gave Me food; I was thirsty and you gave Me drink; I was a stranger and you took Me in; I was naked and you clothed Me; I was sick and you visited Me; I was in prison and you came to Me."
—Matthew 25:34–35

So, how do we go about living this way? The first thing I noticed about this set of instructions is that it requires me to pay attention to the people around me. It's impossible to know if someone is thirsty with a quick glance. We must take the time, first, to observe that person, to ask him what he needs, to get our eyes off our own lives in order to know that he is desperate for a drink.

Secondly, I see action. All of these things are a reaction to someone else's needs. The shepherd sees a need and then moves to meet it. It's not enough to notice that an annoying co-worker is desperate for friends and go about my day. We are called to step into the hurt and show love. If I see that need, I need to take action. I can choose to sit with that co-worker at lunch and start to build a friendship. That's the difference between the sheep and the goats. The goats might notice (or not!), but the sheep notice and step in and do something about the problem.

Are we limited to these things? I can practically hear someone thinking, *"How do I know who I'm supposed to feed? I don't even know anyone who's in jail! Am I supposed to start hanging out at the hospital more, visiting every patient?"*

If that's what you're thinking, you're missing the point. It isn't about checking these specific boxes. Agape means that we follow the example of the shepherd. We pay attention to those around us and then move to meet their needs just as Jesus performs millions of little miracles in our lives daily. There's a moving truck outside a neighbor's house; you walk over and help move some boxes inside or bring a plate of cookies and invite the new family over for supper. A couple in your small group is dealing with marriage problems; you volunteer to watch their kids for a few hours so they can go to dinner and have time alone to talk. As a pastor, I see the sacrifice so many make by simply doing ministry like working with the children or youth. Some serve in cleaning or feeding ministries that have very little, if any, rewards. The rewards are agape rewards. It is a reward to truly worship Christ by serving others as unto Christ. Be warned: this kind of action expects nothing in return.

It just so happens that I own a lot of hammers. Every time I'm at a yard sale and I see one for a dollar or a quarter, I buy it. For some reason, people ask me if they can borrow a hammer or shovel fairly regularly. Do I get those back? Usually not. Knowing this, I've started picking up extras so that I can generously lend them out without worrying about if they're returned or not.

If your expectation when you show someone love is that it will be reciprocated, you're not showing agape. Jesus died for those who never accepted His sacrifice just as much as He died for the sins of those who do. Showing love without expecting anything back frees us to love extravagantly. We understand that God will meet our deeper needs and so, if we are rejected or drained in our attempts to show agape, it's okay. The ultimate goal isn't to promote ourselves; it's to promote God's kingdom.

So far, I have given you very middle-class, nice, easy examples of loving and helping others, but this isn't the kind of radical agape I've learned to live. It's also taking people into my home (obviously with wisdom and caution). We have taken in and are currently taking in people. Maybe it's because of domestic violence, maybe it's to get clean from drugs, maybe it's because of someone's bad choices or from a fire or disaster of some type. Maybe you can't or don't feel safe giving shelter to a stranger, but you can provide it through your church or local outreach. Or maybe there's another form of agape God is calling you to express to your communities around you.

The sad thing is not only do most Christians not reach out with unconditional, tangible love, but many of our churches don't, either. Too many churches only reach out to their members, only willing to help those who are or potentially will help them monetarily. This is not agape love. I understand the economics of it, but faith in Christ isn't built on the worldly economic system. It is based on trusting God to provide whenever He says to go do agape.

I am not telling you to be impulsive, but do be led by the Spirit. When you give to someone who can give you something back, your reward is nothing. At most, it is what they give you. This is not a supernatural love. It is simply a natural love, because natural love only gives natural love. When we begin to love with supernatural love (agape) our reward becomes that which the world cannot give. Luke 6:27–36, Matthew 6:1–10, and Galatians 6:17–

10 make this clear (along with many other scriptures). When you give to someone who can give nothing in return, you then have great rewards come from your source.

The Love Chapter

> *Love suffers long and is kind; love does not envy; love does not parade itself, is not puffed up; does not behave rudely, does not seek its own, is not provoked, thinks no evil; does not rejoice in iniquity, but rejoices in the truth; bears all things, believes all things, hopes all things, endures all things.*
>
> *Love never fails.*
> **—1 Corinthians 13:4–8a**

As we did earlier in the book don't forget to simply add the question, *"Do I love like this?"* after every statement about love. This is a real world, everyday test to determine if you are loving your God, your family, your neighbor, or a stranger with agape. After every action ask yourself, *"Was that agape?"*

How often do we say something we shouldn't, then apologize after the fact? The goal is to temper what you say with agape *before* you say it. That means before you blurt out the unfruitful things out of your mouth, ask yourself, *"Is this agape?"* Truth spoken in agape, brings restoration. If we speak the truth without agape, we may be right (correct about the situation) but still in the wrong. This is how we can speak while still being very wrong!

In all situations, we need to ask if what we are doing or saying is agape. Actions done through agape are often counterintuitive and countercultural. It might be tempting to tell someone off, but is that in accordance with these guidelines? Until I can be kind, humble, and not easily provoked, the answer is no. That person's behavior might need to be addressed, but I must do it with agape.

I think that some people mistake agape with becoming a doormat. God has given each of us responsibilities. We aren't to ignore our families or jobs in order to love others, for example. These responsibilities need to be priorities in our lives. God might call us to set them aside temporarily from time to time in order to love someone, but then we return to them.

We have a really wonderful example to study: Jesus. The more time we spend reading the Gospels, the better we can understand what it looks like to love people in the way that is spelled out in 1 Corinthians 13. Jesus saw the hurting people around Him and stepped in to help. He prioritized spending time with God, often going off on His own to pray. When challenged by the Pharisees, Jesus didn't back down meekly, but gently presented His side of things. And when the time came, He accepted the will of the Father and endured terrible suffering for the good of all humanity.

Agape at times, can seem overwhelming but it isn't complicated. The good news is that we have the Holy Spirit to help us discern what the right thing to do is in each situation. Should I stay in this job where my boss is quick to get on me for every little mistake? If I stay and "bear all things" (1 Corinthians 13:7), is that healthy? If I leave, am I just running away? Go to God, ask, and wait for an answer.

Love Hurts

When I was in the first grade, I remember writing a little note to a girl asking if she loved me. On the note, I made two options—a check box that said yes and a check box that said no. I was afraid of what the answer might be, so in fear of rejection I added another choice. I added a maybe check box. I guess I felt that third option left room for future hope.

In the sixth grade, not much changed. The main difference was I could use our kitchen rotary phone. There was a girl I was interested in, so I called her up to ask if we could date. I wasn't sure where we were going to go. In fact, my mom would have been very against me dating at that age. I am sure she wasn't even in favor of a phone call to a girl in the sixth grade. This girl's response was unexpected. She said, "Let me ask my mom." The answer from her very wise mother was, "No, you cannot." She quickly hung up the phone. Needless to say, I was disappointed.

In all honesty, I didn't really know much about what it meant to love someone or make that kind of commitment. Yet my heart truly cried out to love and be loved. Most of our hearts do. At the same time, our desire for love can leave us vulnerable to the possibility of rejection and pain.

When we examine Jesus' example, we can also learn that love hurts. Agape is a high calling, and it requires a heavy price. I truly believe that it isn't agape love it if doesn't hurt sometimes. Love truly has a cost to it—a cost to our pride, to our time, and ultimately to our comfort.

Jesus was surrounded by disciples who didn't understand what He was saying much of the time. He was hated by the Pharisees and other religious leaders.

This is a fascinating paradox. The world craves agape, but it also rejects those who love that way. We are hardwired to want a relationship with a Holy God. However, to be in relationship with Him means that we give up control of our lives. These two things war within us.

If you are ready to step out and begin to love people, be prepared for this. You won't be the most popular person. You might get passed over for promotions. You might be asked to do more work than other people are asked to do. The people you show agape to might reject you and walk away. No matter how well you're walking with God, that hurts.

Be comforted in knowing that Jesus walked where you did. He experienced the same rejection and loneliness. You can pray knowing that our God not only knows what you're going through but went through it as well. And He went through that suffering because of His agape for you. Second Corinthians 1:5 assures us, "For as the sufferings of Christ abound in us, so our consolation also abounds through Christ."

The fruit of agape relationships comes in relationship with people and, most importantly, a genuine relationship with God. It feels horrible when you have wealth or position and your friends try to get something from you. Give just to give, knowing your source is Jesus and no one else. Love the way you want to be loved. This opens up heaven in a way that is supernatural, and your needs are truly met. Only you know your motives. Are your motives agape? You cannot lose eternally if you are receiving and giving God's love! It's supernatural.

Chapter Seven Questions

Question: Are you paying attention to the needs of those around you? What do you know about your neighbors, coworkers, even your family members? Can you name their hurts, fears, needs, or dreams? If not, what are some actions you can take to build a meaningful relationship based on awareness and understanding?

_____

_____

_____

_____

_____

_____

_____

_____

_____

Question: How is *showing agape love* different from *being nice*? Why do you think that our culture often equates these two ideas? What does the Bible say? What are examples of showing agape love that might even offend or upset the person loved? How has God promise to reward agape in your life? Does He pour into you? How can you pour into others?

_____

_____

_____

_____

_____

_____

_____

_____

Memorize and Personalize: Read John 14 and 15. How does following Jesus' example and obedience to Him relate to love? What is the Holy Spirit's role? What is the world's response? Memorize John 15:12–13 and journal about how you can lay down your life (in most circumstances this is not literal, but your time, energy, preferences, etc.) for those God has called you to love.

_____

_____

_____

_____

_____

_____

_____

_____

_____

_____

Further Study: Study the story of the Prodigal Son in Luke 15. How did the father demonstrate love to both of his sons? How was that love repaid by hurt and betrayal? How does the father exemplify active, need-meeting, self-less love, in spite of the responses of his sons? Evaluate his actions and attitudes by 1 Corinthians 13.

_____

_____

_____

_____

_____

_____

_____

_____

_____

Chapter Seven Notes

CHAPTER EIGHT

Resembling Our Father

I remember when my oldest biological child was born. It was especially thrilling for me because I was adopted. I had adopted my nephew and always cared for him like my own son. However, this was different, because I never had anyone in my life who I could say I resembled. This little girl was the first chance I ever had to meet one of my blood relatives. At that time, I had not even seen a picture of a blood relative. I was dying to find out if she would look like me or act like me. Would we have the same mannerisms? The same earlobes? The same tastes? She definitely may not share the same excitement now that I did then, but you can tell that beautiful girl is my daughter.

Being adopted is such a complicated thing. Genetically, I was related to a group of people who, at that time, I had not met. There were so many questions about myself that had gone unanswered at that time. Now I have the privilege of being in relationship with my birth family, but when my daughter was born, I had never seen anyone that

I could say honestly looked like me.

Inherently, I am similar to my blood relatives. However, I am also like my adopted family. I have the same mannerisms as my adoptive father because we've spent thousands of hours together. There are foods I love because my adoptive mother cooked them all the time growing up. Over the years, I have become more like my adoptive family than my birth family. Although I still share a genetic makeup with them, we're not alike in so many other ways, although very alike in others.

Like Jesus

There are places throughout the New Testament that refer to our new life in Christ as being adopted into God's family. Once we are adopted, the expectation is that we start spending time with our new Father and become more and more like Him. We have to choose to reflect Christ, because we have spent time in His Word and in prayer.

Sure, we still have the same inborn tendencies for sinful behavior. We still have the same past that we did before. However, now we also have a new inheritance. I might have the genetic predisposition that leans towards alcoholism, but my adoptive family might be one that doesn't drink alcohol and teaches me to deal with life's challenges in healthier ways.

Similarly, as we spend time with God, the expectation is that we become more like Him. Jesus is the perfect example of this. There is no moment in His life that doesn't perfectly reflect God's nature. In the Gospels, Jesus goes off on His own to spend time in prayer repeatedly. He spends time with the Father and then also reflects the Father in all of His interactions with people.

Agape Ain't Easy, It's Family

The closer we grow to people, the harder it is to love with agape. It's not difficult to have a moment of generosity or selflessness. I might not be overly happy about missing the football game, but I feel good that I served someone else for a short period of time. Is that feeling of charity my reward? Am I doing it unto Jesus or trying to remove a little guilt?

It's much harder to invite people into our lives and love them with agape right where we live. Look at it as an investment into the kingdom of God that will change lives as we pour out our love for Christ. When we grow close to people and let them grow close to us, it becomes impossible to hide our sinful ways. As people matter more to us, their rejection packs more of a punch. If a coworker I'm trying to build a relationship with ditches me when we planned to meet, it might be annoying. If my wife Kristy ditches me, I'm going to be deeply hurt.

People are so incredibly hungry for God. They are drawn, or at least should be drawn, to followers of Christ because of our agape. God's love never fails, but unfortunately, His people often do. When someone searching for God is disappointed or hurt by one of His followers, it's even more of a blow. My selfishness can have eternal consequences and that is a heavy responsibility. It's incredibly important that we grow in our understanding of agape so that we can reach others for God's kingdom! We represent God's family because we have been grafted in.

First John 3:1 says, "Behold what manner of love the Father has bestowed on us, that we should be called children of God! Therefore, the world does not know us, because it did not know Him." God has freely given (bestowed) His agape to those who have chosen to follow Him. If someone hasn't chosen to follow God, they won't experience His agape to the same extent. They cannot, because—while we all can show many different kinds of love—there is only one love, fruit that tastes like Jesus, reveals Jesus, and causes everlasting change.

My wife and I have had the opportunity to travel to many countries with all of our children. On our last trip to Africa, while in Kenya, my son Maverick (eleven years old at the time) asked me if he could preach something in one of the jungle village churches. I asked him a few questions and said yes. He did a fabulous job and has ministered with me on many other occasions. A few days later, we were at a meeting and were feeding people. My daughter Eva (eight years old at the time) suddenly slipped away and in a panic, I began to look for her. Within a few seconds I found her with her plate of food and a line of children. She was feeding the hungry children off of her own plate of food. What could I say? Nothing. I just teared up.

In their own way, they both were ministering the love of God. When we returned home, the greatest impact wasn't the great preaching of "Aaron Taylor" or my amazing wife Kristy. Oh no, the lasting effects on the church, people, and orphanages were the ministry of my precious children and their overwhelming love for others. Every time I speak to one of my pastor friends from Africa or the Philippines, they always ask me, "How are those amazing children of yours?" simply because at a young age they agape. It's not so much taught, it's caught.

Many are affected by agape and even emulate it, but when people receive it and it gives them a revelation or realization of Jesus, *that's* the overwhelming, supernatural power of true unconditional love.

We, as God's children, are called to love the world. When you read through the book of Acts, you see that this call is a costly one. The disciples sacrificed their comfort, their reputations, their freedom, and even their lives as they answered God's call. We are the ones who have received the fullness of God's agape, and we are expected to emulate that in our dealings with the world around us.

However, the world isn't equipped to love us back and we shouldn't expect them to. In fact, we often share the gospel message in a manner like we are trying to save someone. In all reality, I cannot adopt someone into the family—only God can. I cannot save someone from their sins or make them born again of the Spirit of God—only God can. In fact, without God's help and enabling grace, we cannot even truly agape someone. Agape isn't easy but it allows us to add to the family of God. Love isn't always easy but it's always about family. Even when you reach out to a stranger, it's about family. Read the parable of the Good Samaritan, in Luke 10, with this aspect of agape in mind.

Agape Is a Covenant

I can hear some of you saying, "Okay, Pastor, so what does it look like to love the way God does?" There are three key things I want to point out in this chapter.

First, we need to reset our understanding of what love is. In our modern American culture, love is a feeling. It's fluid. It comes and goes like the waves on the beach. We think that we can't help who we love or don't love. We think love is tolerant and permissive. Maybe that describes eros or phileo, but that isn't what agape love is.

We see love as an emotion. Emotions are a product of the soul of a person. Agape is a product of the Spirit given to and leading the soul which causes the body to come into obedience to God. The point is that the Spirit of God within a man is supposed to lead a man's soul. Emotions are a soul thing, while agape is a Spirit thing. Does it matter? Yes, it makes a big difference. There is a difference between being led by your emotions and being led by the Spirit of God.

Remember that *God* is a covenant *keeper*. Even to the point of sacrificing His own son, God keeps His promises. As we read through the Old Testament, we see that God is a warrior who fiercely defends His people. He doesn't hesitate to wipe out evil when He chooses (see what happened to Korah in Numbers 16!). Agape demands justice. It never fails.

Conversely, *we* are covenant *breakers*. We are quick to give in whenever we are so inclined. As we grow more like our Father, we should see ourselves becoming covenant keepers more and more. We will spend time learning what it is that God is calling us to do and go forward willingly. We will see our neighbors and colleagues as our responsibility to love. Then, even when we take a hit, we keep on fighting God's fight.

God's covenant between Himself and Abraham is surely the greatest covenant of all. It was the covenant that brought us salvation as we know it. God was saying, in effect, "Because we are joined in this covenant, if I fail the covenant, I will be cut in two, and if you fail the covenant, I will be cut in two." Jesus was the one who paid the full price of that broken covenant when He became the Lamb of God on the cross.

God made a covenant of love and kept that covenant of love when on the cross. We see a true separation of Jesus and the Father as the Father turned His back on the Lamb who became sin for us. Agape is when you pay the price for someone else's failure.

Fear and Love Can't Coexist

I've met many people who've admitted to me that they struggle with the fear of God's judgment. Like Adam and Eve in the Garden of Eden, they try to keep God from drawing close and seeing their sin. But keeping God at arm's length also means that we aren't basking in the fullness of His incredible agape.

God sees everything. There is nothing that can be hidden from Him. Mark 4:22 tells us, "For there is nothing hidden which will not be revealed, nor has anything been kept secret but that it should come to light." God knows our motives, our extenuating circumstances, our secret desires. There is no hiding from Him. That's really wonderful news for everyone who's been made to feel ashamed for being victimized. The acts of our abusers will be brought to light and paid for.

Yet, those words are also frightening to many Christians. I surely do not want my sins laid out for all to see. However, there is good news for us, too. "Most assuredly, I say to you, he who hears My word and believes in Him who sent Me has everlasting life, and shall not come into judgment, but has passed from death into life" (John 5:24). On the day of judgment, when we stand before God, He won't look at our sin record; He'll look at His Son's perfect record. Jesus paid the debt for my sins so that I don't have to.

You can confidently walk into God's presence and not be afraid of His wrath. With childlike confidence, you can skip into His court and climb onto His lap and tell your Heavenly Father whatever is on your heart.

There are a number of adorable photographs of John F. Kennedy Jr. as a little boy playing under his father's desk in the Oval Office. I don't know about you, but if I were called to the Oval Office to be in the presence of the president of the United States, I would be nervous at the very least. This is the most powerful man in our government! If I mess up, he can make my life miserable! But for little JFK Jr., the president was just his dad. He might be dealing with international decisions at his desk, but his son was playing happily at his feet.

If you, who are already wiped clean by the blood of Christ, feel overwhelmed at the thought of drawing near to God, how much more so must your unsaved friends fear? Part of agape is growing close to other people then gently taking them by the hand and helping them to draw near to God together. We cannot do that if we fear Him. First John 4:18 reassures us, "There is no fear in love; but perfect love casts out fear."

We don't have to fear God's judgment. And, in return, the people we love with agape shouldn't fear our judgment. That doesn't mean we don't hold people accountable. No, agape love doesn't tolerate sin. It does mean we keep loving through sin. If my daughter lies to me, I'm going to have to discipline her. I'm not going to stop loving her. Our agape should never be used as leverage to discipline. Threat of rejection isn't good discipline at all. Our love should never be optional. Loving correction is never rejection, or even a threat of rejection.

God's love was extended to me while I was a sinner and through any failure, He chooses to love me and draw me with His love. When my co-worker tells me he doesn't want anything to do with God or me, I'm not going to stop loving him. I might have to set some boundaries, but I'm going to be praying even harder for him and do my best to show him love.

Agape Is Unconditional

When I was a young Christian, I had a very limited understanding of agape. I found it easy to love people who loved me back. Certain members of the church just naturally clicked with me, and it was a delight to step in and generously help them when they needed it. In the beginning of our relationship, I was thrilled to lend a hand to my wife if she needed it.

But my commitment to agape was sorely tested when

the person I was called to love couldn't reciprocate. That family was facing *another* crisis and I had to save the day *again*. I wanted to spend some time alone with my wife, but she'd had a bad day and needed some space. I wanted to throw up my hands and play the victim card; *she's* the one who's making it impossible to love her! I'm putting in the effort, but *they* aren't interested in God! I've done what I can and I'm going to give up!

Here's the thing about agape: it's only when you love somebody who cannot do anything for you that you are showing agape love. That is when we can show mercy, patience, and kindness.

It's how God loves us, isn't it? And over time, as we grow closer to Him, we are able to start loving Him unconditionally, too. We stop saying, "I'll only love you so long as I get this desire of my heart," and we start saying, "Father, what is the desire of Your heart for me and also for them?" We stop demanding that God meets our expectations in order for us to love Him. As we receive God's unconditional love, we are able to then love Him and others unconditionally.

Love Until It Hurts

I hope there are two things you take away from this chapter. First, we must spend time with God. Secondly, don't expect people to perfectly reciprocate agape. Agape love isn't the sort of thing where I pour love into someone's cup and that person then pours the same amount of love back into my cup.

Instead, we draw closer to God who fills all our needy

places to overflowing. In gratefulness, we then turn and pour ourselves out, filling the cups around us. We don't worry that we'll run dry because we can always return to the place where we are refilled—a well that never runs dry.

This is what allows me to work with people in great need because I go back to my need for the Lord. It lends me far more patience to deal with difficulty than I would ever have on my own. This doesn't mean that we put ourselves into abusive situations. Healthy boundaries are crucial to loving others. Some relationships are not healthy, or the other person will walk away, but you never have to stop forgiving and loving that person. It's not your job to save anyone; it's your job to point the way to God with your love, to extend the fruit of love and all the fruits of the Spirit.

Chapter Eight Questions

Question: In what ways has fear tainted your relationship with God? How does understanding His love answer that fear? Can agape love help heal fear in human relationships? Why or why not?

_____

_____

_____

_____

_____

_____

_____

_____

_____

Question: *It's only when you love somebody who cannot do anything for you that you are showing agape love.* Is your love for God based on what He gives you or Who He is? How about your love for others? What commitments have you made (e.g., marriage vows) and do these commitments inform and empower your love?

_____

_____

_____

_____

_____

_____

_____

_____

_____

Memorize and Personalize: Memorize 1 John 4:16–21. How does John show the connection between loving God and loving others?

_____

_____

_____

_____

_____

_____

_____

_____

_____

_____

Further Study: Study the book of 1 John. A commentary or study guide will help you to go deeper and understand the context. As you study and pray through this short, powerful epistle, journal what it teaches about God's love and about love for others.

_____

_____

_____

_____

_____

_____

_____

_____

_____

_____

_____

Chapter Eight Notes

CHAPTER NINE

When Love Fails

Let's say I've convinced you to start striving more toward loving with agape. Off you go, enthusiastic and eager to change the world. Things might go really well that first week, that first day, and that first hour.

But eventually you're going to come up against something that causes your love to fail. It's inevitable. Life has so many curve balls. Sometimes it's us. sometimes it's others.

One thing is for sure—our love does fail. The proverbial "woke up on the wrong side of the bed" excuse and the "if you then I" excuse, and others like them, all have real world consequences. In this world, you will have trials of many kinds. They come with many judges and juries. There is only one Judge who matters and He's the one pouring out the love. *Do you love?*

You can't beat yourself up when you fail. You just have to move ahead in repentance. Repentance doesn't just mean saying, "I am sorry." It means saying, "I will bring about change with God's grace. I will turn away from what was wrong and turn to what is right."

Your failure to agape may be simple. It may seem to affect no one, but did it? Our children are often products of our failure to agape. I honestly believe every parent at one time or another is bombarded by the enemy with guilt and shame. We have to rise out of that and simply return to agape. Just go back to loving. "I failed but I refuse to be a failure at love!" Then do your best and let God love through you.

After one of the most difficult times in my life, my father gave me some of the best advice that has seen me through so much. I will never forget him asking, "What are you going to do? Quit? Give up?"

I responded, "I don't know."

"Son, there is really only one thing to do. Lift your head up, listen to what the Lord says about you and not other people, then go forward."

Those words touched me deeply and I always come back to them in times of difficulty. Those words help me continue to pursue agape.

One of the most tragic moments in my life came when I was trying to balance family and ministry. I was trying to be there for everyone, and my family was suffering. I decided that if people wanted to speak with me, they would have to set an appointment. It seemed very reasonable but, in all honesty, it was out of frustration.

We may make rules to live by, but we always need to be led by the Spirit. Even in our rules, we have to show love. I had determined my rules. The first day didn't go so well. It was getting late, and I needed to leave the office.

A lady came to my office as I was leaving and said, "Pastor, I have been watching you preach the Bible on television. I really have some problems I need to discuss with someone."

Somewhat reluctant but determined, I said, "I am sorry you will need to schedule an appointment with the person in the office next to mine."

She was obviously disturbed by my response and said, "Well, never mind."

My compassion broke my determination and I said, "Okay, okay. If it's important, I will meet with you for a few minutes."

She was obviously emotional and feeling rejected and said, "No! It's fine!" She left my office, drove down the street and shot herself.

Trying to console me, many say, "Well, you did all you could do." The truth was that in a time of frustration with myself and self-made demands, I responded to her in the flesh. I didn't win that day. She didn't win that day. Agape didn't rule the day. I failed the test of love that day, and it had very disturbing consequences. I can make lots of excuses to try and console myself. But in reality, I couldn't see past my own frustration to see her real need. It was an urgent need, a three-alarm "something needs to happen now" kind of need. I could have responded with much more love and compassion. I didn't.

I may have failed, but that failure cannot rule the day, my future, or my life. I have to choose to lift my head up, repent of my lack of choosing agape, and live another day closer to the Lord than before.

Maybe if I had stopped and listened to the urging of the

Spirit that day, we all could have won and rejoiced together. What I do know is I have chosen to cling to the One who enables me to simply be more fruitful and sensitive. I want to be less determined to accomplish and more deliberate to agape.

We need to keep in mind: *we may fail to love but love never fails.*

It never quits. Agape is eternal. It lasts the test of time. When you love as unto the Lord, it cannot go unnoticed. It will never fail to have great significance if you see the fruit of it or not.

Agape Love Can't Fail

What I'm going to say next is deep and can be a little confusing, but please stick with me. You see, agape can't fail. By definition, it is impossible. First Corinthians 13:8a says, "Love never fails" (NIV). When we think of God as loving us with agape, knowing that His love cannot fail is extremely comforting. No matter what we do, God's love won't fail us.

When it comes to our attempts to love, though, it's possible to fail. We are fallible. It's in our sinful nature, hardwired into us at the most basic level. It's tempting to look at that, throw up our hands, and say, "Well, that's it for me. I can't achieve this. I can't love with agape."

Let me show you this in another way. God is sinless. He calls us to be sinless, too (Matthew 5:48). Yet, we have failed there in big ways, right? However, when we are walking in relationship with the Holy Spirit, we have the ability to see the temptation of sin more clearly and choose to avoid it. There are times when we choose to walk with God and avoid sin.

But there's another interesting piece of the puzzle that we need to consider. In order for love to be agape love, it must have the potential to fail.

In the Garden of Eden, God placed the Tree of the Knowledge of Good and Evil. Why did He do that? It sure didn't take long before Eve plucked that fruit and shared it with Adam. Wouldn't it have made more sense to remove that temptation?

There's a fundamental principle at work here—love isn't love if you don't have a choice. If it's forced, it isn't love. One of the amazing aspects of agape is that it is so impossibly perfect. When we see a human do an extraordinary act of agape, we are all drawn to it. It is more awesome and powerful because it is so difficult to achieve.

There will be times when we choose to walk with God and love with agape. We will fail, but there is always the opportunity to get back up and move forward, growing in our ability to show agape to the people around us.

Is My Love Failing?

In my experience, there are times when we charge forward, thinking we're loving with agape when, in truth, we're missing the mark. If we stop and reflect, we often know in our spirits that something isn't right. However, we don't always like to take the time to reflect or listen to that nagging voice which tells us that something is off.

So, let's look at some common failings of agape, both

in our relationships with God and with others.

First of all, agape doesn't have contingencies. It doesn't depend on someone else meeting a certain set of criteria. I think this is something we do both to God and other people. We say to our friends, "I'll love you and be there for you unless you do something I don't like, or you stop reciprocating." We say to God, "I'll love and serve You, but don't ask me to do anything too difficult. You are my God so long as my life goes smoothly, and I get the things I want."

Agape doesn't do that. It sets boundaries, yes. It takes time to rest. It doesn't enable others' bad choices. However, it sacrifices our agendas for God's agenda. We are asked to lay down our dreams and pick up God's dreams. We are to worship God, not comfort or ambition. In any situation where we are asked to love in big ways, I find it helpful to ask myself, *"What can I reasonably do?"* Often, the Holy Spirit prompts me to step in and use my gifts to love others and obey God in ways I wouldn't have on my own.

Secondly, agape gives us enormous freedom which must be used in obedience to God. Galatians 5:13 says, "For you, brethren, have been called to liberty; only do not use liberty as an opportunity for the flesh."

Because of God's agape, Jesus died on the cross, which allows our sins to be cancelled. No longer do we have to live in guilt or shame because our sins have been struck from the record. The old laws no longer apply.

In the Apostle Paul's days, this caused some big problems. Some Christians took this to mean that it was fine to sin because it would all be forgiven. Paul had to address that both with the Galatians and the Corinthians.

When we grow closer to God, we desire to obey Him more and more. Sinful things are less desirable to us. We start wanting to treat people around us in a way that points to Jesus. Things that are tainted by sin are less appealing to us.

If you are loving someone and there is something sinful in your heart toward them, you are not loving with agape. There's someone in your small group who makes you roll your eyes impatiently every time she opens her mouth. That's not agape. You grow angry with God every time you think about the fact you aren't married yet. That's not agape. You know you should go over and speak with your neighbor when he's out playing with his kids in the yard, but you'd really rather watch football. That's not agape. Hear Jesus saying, "Do you love Me? Then feed My little ones, My sheep. Take care of the least of these."

Agape isn't just about what you receive from God. Sometimes I grow weary of listening to Christian music because so many of the songs we most love focus only on how God loves us. Don't get me wrong: that's a beautiful, incredible, mind-blowing thing!

But modern American Christians get into the habit of thinking that church is "all about me." We want the music to be to our taste, the sermons to touch our hearts, and the coffee to be from our favorite place. Our consumerism has tainted our view of agape.

Receiving agape love and doing nothing with it isn't agape. There is a natural response in our hearts that must take this love and then pour it out on others. If someone claims to be in a relationship with God yet takes no action, it isn't agape.

Finding Your Way Back to Love

When I read the line "love never fails," I'm often struck with the knowledge that I'm not going to be able to ever live up to that. Similarly, when I read that I'm called to a life of holiness, it's overwhelmingly impossible.

But I'm also extremely encouraged by the lives of the disciples. When I look at the difference in them before and after the giving of the Spirit, I'm astounded. The Apostles in Acts seem like completely different men from the ones in the Gospels. Before Jesus sent the Holy Spirit to abide in us as born-again believers, Peter denied knowing Him three times (Luke 22:54–62). Afterwards, Peter gave his life for the sake of the gospel.

When you struggle to love people, look to the cross. Remember that our God set an example for us of perfect love. His death allows us both to experience agape fully and to give it to others. Instead of assuming you are going to fail, set your heart on striving to achieve it. Always remember we can love with God's kind of love if we let our flesh stand aside (or die) and let Jesus agape through us.

Again, relationship is the key to agape. If you are in a healthy, growing relationship with God, you will be led by the Holy Spirit, not your sinful flesh. Even though it would feel good or make you happy to do a sinful thing, being obedient to God takes precedence. The more you find freedom from sin through right relationship with God, the easier it is to love others with agape.

"But the fruit of the spirit is love, joy, peace, longsuf-fering, kindness, goodness, faithfulness, gentleness, self-control. Against such there is no law" (Galatians 5:22–23). If the fruit of the Spirit is growing in you, agape hap-pens more readily. Do you see yourself becoming more patient? Is goodness something you crave? Are you grow-ing in the fruit of the Spirit? If your answer is no, then you have some work to do. Spend time building your relation-ship with God and you'll see the fruit of the Spirit blossoming in your life.

Every one of us has the ability to love. If you know Jesus, you can love with agape. If you don't know Jesus, true supernatural agape is impossible. Any success we have loving with agape isn't due to us, it's because of God. We are merely conduits for agape. Remember His Supply is much greater than our need and our ability.

WORKBOOK

Chapter Nine Questions

Question: Have you ever been in or observed a relationship where one person tried to demand and force love from the other? How was this relationship unhealthy? How is that different from the freedom of God's agape love?

_____

_____

_____

_____

_____

_____

_____

_____

_____

Question: What is the difference between having healthy boundaries and unloving contingencies? What is the difference between walking in the freedom of God's agape love and living in sinful license? What is the difference between rejoicing in God's personal love for you and becoming selfish, or self-centered, in your worship and service?

_____

_____

_____

_____

_____

_____

_____

_____

_____

_____

Memorize and Personalize: Learn the fruit of the Spirit as listed in Galatians 5:22–23. What qualities will follow a life that is full of love? How are you growing in each of these fruits? Do you desire the Holy Spirit to grow these qualities in your life, even if the process is painful?

_____

_____

_____

_____

_____

_____

_____

_____

_____

_____

Further Study: Learn more about how to have a daily devotional time, how to grow in the discipline of personal prayer, or how to build spiritual disciplines into your life. What is one way that you can intentionally grow in your relationship with God?

_____

_____

_____

_____

_____

_____

_____

_____

_____

Chapter Nine Notes

_____

_____

_____

_____

_____

_____

_____

_____

_____

_____

_____

_____

_____

_____

_____

_____

_____

_____

_____

_____

_____

_____

_____

CHAPTER TEN

Forgiveness

The longer we live, the more injustices we've endured. It's just the way the world works. As life goes on, we carry an ever-growing weight of hurt feelings, betrayals, misunderstandings, and abuse, resulting in a lack of trust. Unless we are truly able to forgive, we won't be able to show agape to others.

> *[Love] does not dishonor others, it is not self-seeking, it is not easily angered, it keeps no record of wrongs.*
> **—1 Corinthians 13:5(NIV)**

Forgiveness is a crucial part of agape. It's foundational. God showed His agape to us by sacrificing His son for the forgiveness of our sins. This cosmic sacrifice was done in order to offer forgiveness. It was painful and undeserved, yet agape hinges on it. Forgiveness is not about just freeing someone else because you're not the judge. It's about freeing yourself from being judge and jury. That can be a lot of work, a big responsibility, and an emotional over-load. Let God be that judge. Remember we are judged in our circumstances, according to our judgment of others in theirs. It's us giving our enemy and condemner permission to treat us the way we are treating others

Look back at the verse above to see what we are called to do. First, we are not to be rude and then we are not to be self-seeking. Nor are we to be quick to lose our tempers. When wrong is committed against us, we don't hold on to it. All but true order! Let's apply this to a real-life situation.

Your co-worker is having a bad day. She criticizes the report you just turned in, blatantly calling you out for a mistake you made. It's embarrassing and unjust. How does agape demand we respond? First, don't be rude. No matter what this co-worker says, don't respond with a nasty attitude or unkind sarcasm. Okay, I will admit it, this is not number one—or even on the top ten—of my strong points, but it is God's pattern for showing agape.

Then, don't be self-seeking. Humbly recognize that fixing this problem is for the good of the company and accept the criticism with grace. If the co-worker mumbles under her breath that you shouldn't be given this kind of responsibility, don't lose your temper. Hand that to God each time it comes to mind throughout the day instead of steaming over the incident. And go forward. Like my father said to me, "You lift your head up and move forward."

When you forgive, you allow God in faith to right your wrongs. You don't dredge this back up and whisper it to other co-workers. Let God handle it and be your defender.

Where the Rubber Really Meets the Road

Okay, so that's the nice, middle-class Christian church-goer example. Here is the real world, let-your-guard-down, get real, rubber-meets-road kind of forgiveness. This is the stuff that makes it very hard to forgive, yet it has to be forgiven—the stuff you have to allow God to deal with. This includes sexual and physical abuses and neglect of you or the people you love. It doesn't mean you don't talk with the police or do what needs to be done, but you have to truly forgive.

Agape-level forgiveness is seen in a situation when you or your child is molested. Or when you're trying to forgive yourself or a spouse for aborting your unborn child. It's when you were betrayed by who you thought was your best friend. It's dealing with infidelity from your spouse; maybe it was with another person, or with drugs or alcohol. You are struggling to forgive the person who killed your mother. It could be you are angry at the person who committed suicide and left you alone to raise your children. It could be a divorced spouse or abusive relationship.

Yes, forgiveness is a real thing. It may be needed for a big thing or something small—but it is a choice we have to make for our freedom and sanity. It also has the ability lead to judgment or forgiveness and restoration in Jesus.

I had one man explain to me that he was trying to forgive his father for killing his mother. He said he had to release it every holiday, every kid's sporting event, any situation that reminded him of the lost dynamic. He said,

"The emotion wells up and I have to choose to forgive." Forgiveness in these kinds of extreme situations doesn't mean you have to choose relationship. But it does require you to cast the hurt at the feet of Jesus and to allow Him to bind up your wounds.

The Truth of Forgiveness

Forgiveness is a funny thing. It asks us to look at the truth, not the facts. The facts tell us all the things we've done wrong or have been done wrong to us. By the facts, none of us are innocent. However, the truth is that God has forgiven our sins. If we look at the facts, we are hopelessly lost. The truth, though, tells us that we are saved through Christ. The facts say we will lose our justice if we forgive. The truth is Jesus is always just and His mercy for us and those who have wronged us is greater than our need for justice. Let it go and agape those who have wronged you.

Jesus, on the cross, said to forgive them because they know not what they are doing. He was saying, "They are walking in deception so please forgive them that they might see." We need to realize people not walking in the Spirit are walking in darkness. Christians walk in darkness sometimes, but we are called to light. We need to release those who have wronged us in order to see the light and truth of the gospel rather than try to condemn them to what they deserve. Jesus said to love our enemies. True agape loves the broken and the guilty. It hopes for the best and looks for the salvation of *all*.

Keeping Score

Agape keeps no records of wrongs. We are to let go of the wrongs done to us. I don't know about you but keeping a list of every little hurt doesn't work well for me. It becomes a huge barrier between me and everyone else pretty quickly. Even if we let go of little things and hold onto the big things, we cannot agape the people around us.

Let me make two important points. First, the Bible says we are "not easily angered" (1 Corinthians 13:5 NIV), not that we are never to grow angry. We are called to become angry over injustice, as Jesus was in the temple with the money changers (Matthew 21:12–13). Anger is an emotion and emotions aren't inherently sinful. We should be slow and reluctant to become angry. When we do become angry, we are still called to behave without sin. This means we continue in the fruit of the Spirit—we continue in agape. Anger cannot change or stop the fruit if it's a righteous anger.

Secondly, though we "keep no record of wrongs" (1 Corinthians 13:5, NIV), that doesn't mean we don't learn from the experience. If my daughter yells at me, calling me names and threatening to run away, I can forgive her but still hold her accountable. Forgiving someone for abuse doesn't mean you put yourself back under that person's power. It does mean in faith (trusting God) you put the offense and them under the power of God.

Don't Stop Forgiving

Forgiveness is an ongoing process. It doesn't just need to happen once. You might find that you must forgive the same person for something that happened in the past many times before you are free of it.

Jesus said we are to forgive seventy times seven times (Matthew 18:22), meaning that we are to forgive much longer than the world would expect. We forgive more than we have the physical ability to forgive. This means with supernatural power we forgive and go beyond what we can physically. God gives us this example by forgiving us over and over again. As we understand the enormity of the debt we no longer carry, the natural response is to turn and extend that to others in equal measure.

I want to pause and point out something interesting about the number "seventy times seven." This is more than just 490 times. Seven is considered the number of completion in the Bible. Seventy times seven takes that completion to a higher level. This number represents godly perfection. Forgive by giving it to God and let it be done. Don't carry it any longer.

Therefore, when we're called to forgive "seventy times seven," Jesus meant that we are to forgive with godly perfection as we have been forgiven by God. That can only be completed by Christ's work on the cross. We can only forgive others perfectly through Jesus. We receive the fullness of perfect forgiveness from Christ which enables us to forgive others. We can receive and give the agape of God.

If anyone says, "I love God," but hates his brother, he is a liar. For anyone who does not love his brother, whom he has seen, cannot love God, whom he has not seen. And we have this commandment from Him: Whoever loves God must love his brother as well.

—1 John 4:20–21 *(BSB)*

For if you forgive men their trespasses, your heavenly Father will also forgive you. But if you do not forgive men their trespasses, neither will your Father forgive your trespasses.

—Matthew 6:14–15

These scriptures are two of many that make this clear. It will take forgiveness and agape to be pleasing to the Lord. He gives us the grace (unearned spiritual ability and enabling power of God at work in us) to love. He also has given us mercy (not giving us what we deserve) in our situation to forgive others in their situation. Whether we deem their situation to be bigger or smaller than ours, we can love and forgive.

The Role of Repentance

All sins have been paid for, but until we accept this forgiveness, we still carry the record of them. When we forgive others, we don't erase their wrongs, we stop carrying them around with us. We forgive their debts and stop expecting them to repay us. Sounds a little like this agape we have been reading about, doesn't it? That's because it is agape. God still holds the person accountable, and the sin still requires payment. It may be through His forgiveness, sowing and reaping in this life, and/or through eternal separation from God. It is between them and God, because our place is of the forgiven, not the judge.

There are times when it's hard to forgive someone without seeing some sort of justice. When huge wrongs are committed, it's tempting to withhold forgiveness, believing we are somehow punishing the person who sinned against us. It's not our job, though, to exact payment. Refusing to forgive does nothing but let the wound fester.

We must repent to God in order to be forgiven, but others don't need to repent to us in order for us to forgive them. At first, that seems skewed. But your role in forgiveness isn't the same as God's. The sin, though it affected you, isn't really against you. All sin is against God. Any debt incurred is owed to Him. We don't need the other party to be sorry for the wrong done us in order for us to let go of it. They don't even need to ask for forgiveness and maybe they can't.

What is wonderful about this is that our forgiveness of others can lead them to repentance and right standing with God. Some people hurt others and think nothing of it. In other instances, the wrong done haunts the person who committed it. When we are able to forgive extravagantly, we demonstrate God's forgiveness and that can draw people to Christ. Your act of forgiving can change eternity. Your act of forgiveness is truly agape in action. When you love without condition, expecting nothing in return, forgiveness is made possible. You do it as unto the Lord, the one who forgave you. Instead of a dreadful act, it is an exciting and freeing thing to do. Whoever you hold an offence with, go now and forgive them that your gifts towards God may be acceptable!

> *Therefore if you bring your gift to the altar, and there remember that your brother has something against you, leave your gift there before the altar, and go your way. First be reconciled to your brother, and then come and offer your gift.*
> **—Matthew 5:23–24**

I know I have said you don't always have to reconcile the relationship but when it is possible, we need to. Reconciliation simply means to come back into right relationship with someone. Sometimes we feel like we cannot ever reconcile with someone who we have offended or who has offended us. If we start with loving and forgiving as unto the Lord, anything is possible. Lord, let our life and gifts be acceptable.

Although I talk about forgiveness in this book, it isn't solely about forgiveness. That being said, I can't leave this chapter without saying that although we must grant forgiveness, that doesn't mean we have to trust. Forgiveness is something we must choose. It grants us the freedom we need to walk in love. We do not have to trust. Trust is earned. We can choose to risk, but we need a track record to trust. You can choose to forgive, and when you choose to agape, a door can open for trust to grow. Free them with forgiveness, but don't hold them to an expectation, because you are unable to show perfect love.

WORKBOOK

Chapter Ten Questions

Question: Do you tend to let things go or to keep a record of wrongs done against you? Is there anyone that you have a "mental list" against? Why do you feel that you have to keep track of these offenses? In what situations do you find it most difficult to stop keeping a record of wrongs?

_____

_____

_____

_____

_____

_____

_____

_____

_____

Question: Describe a time when you had to forgive a person more than once for the same offense, either because they repeated it or because you were still working through the process of forgiveness in your own heart. How does understanding Christ's forgiveness of you help you to forgive others even when they aren't repentant?

_____

_____

_____

_____

_____

_____

_____

_____

_____

Memorize and Personalize: Memorize Ephesians 4:32–5:2. What do these verses teach about who you are in Christ and how He has loved you? In what situations right now could your forgiveness of another person point them to God?

_____

_____

_____

_____

_____

_____

_____

_____

_____

_____

Further Study: Read or watch an interview with a person who has chosen to forgive someone who committed a crime against them or their loved one. Why was forgiveness impossible at a human level? What helped the victim to forgive? How did their choice to forgive testify to the world of Christ's love?

_____

_____

_____

_____

_____

_____

_____

_____

_____

Chapter Ten Notes

CHAPTER ELEVEN

What Seeds Are You Planting?

The land is threatened by a fire-breathing dragon that is destroying everything and has kidnapped the king. A stalwart group of knights has banded together. They are the kingdom's only hope!

However, when the time comes for them to set out and begin their quest, one of the knights looks around at his comfortable house and says, "Nah, you guys go ahead without me. I'm going to stay here."

How selfish!

Yet, we do the same thing. I wonder how many people will read this book, be convinced of the message, and still make no changes in their lives. How many will opt out of the quest of agape? Will you continue to answer, like Peter, "I phileo" to Jesus when He asks, "Is that agape?"

Will we go out and love others with agape? Love those who can give us nothing in return? Without expectation?

It's a big ask! Jesus showed Peter how to agape Him. On the day of Pentecost—when he stood up and spoke the gospel message—we see the fruit of an agape life in Peter. It's evident throughout the book of Acts—and in Peter's death, when he gave his life in crucifixion so that others might hear the gospel.

Some consider the price of agape too high, and we see them turn away. I hope this will not be you. I hope you will choose to live a life of sacrifice that others may know, that others may live, that others may taste and see that the fruit of agape is very good. Jesus is agape; let the world taste Him through you. Plant the seeds of agape in your life then watch them grow into something beautiful. Remember, agape is a fruit of the Spirit, and fruits have seeds. When you love like Jesus, you can't help but plant seeds. Not all seeds take root, but all good seeds have the potential to reproduce. When we agape, we give real life a chance to grow in someone and in our relationships.

The Rich Young Ruler

One day, a wealthy man approached Jesus. He respectfully asked Jesus what he needed to do in order to achieve eternal life. Jesus said:

> *"You know the commandments: 'Do not commit adultery,' 'Do not murder,' 'Do not steal,' 'Do not bear false witness,' 'Do not defraud,' 'Honor your father and your mother.'"*

> *And [the young man] answered and said to Him, "Teacher, all these things I have kept from my youth."*

> *Then Jesus, looking at him, loved him, and said to him, "One thing you lack: Go your way, sell whatever you have and*

give to the poor, and you will have treasure in heaven; and come, take up the cross, and follow Me."

But [the young man] was sad at this word, and went away sorrowful, for he had great possessions.
—Mark 10:19–22

Jesus understood what was happening in this man's heart. The problem wasn't that the young ruler had possessions. The problem was that his possessions had him. The young man was dependent on something other than God.

Let's not judge this man too harshly. After all, we do the same thing. We depend on money, friends, abilities, appearance, or power to fill us with meaning. They become our identity and we can't imagine being separated from them.

I've seen so many people walk away from their faith in God who tell me that He let them down. God didn't provide for them what they thought He would. However, often I do a little probing and learn that these people never let go of the baggage they brought with them. "Kate" expected God to forgive her past, but she refused to let go of it herself. "Pete" wanted to no longer feel guilty, but he never gave up his shameful sin habits. "Susan" was desperate to stop feeling empty and meaningless, but she kept pursuing things that drained her life with no real return.

Like this rich young ruler, we tend to want eternal life without giving up control of our lives to Jesus. We like the idea of heaven but don't like the pathway to get there ourselves or bring others with us. We show with our lives that we think, *"If loving people with agape means I have to give up my schedule and watching my shows and spending money on myself, I'm not interested."* We've chosen these bags, stuffed them full of meaningless stuff, and now refuse to put them down so we can pick up something infinitely valuable.

The Return on Your Investment

Imagine that you have a reservoir inside of you. This is where you dip to find everything you need for your life. It's where you find purpose, hope, courage, and love. You have the choice as to what you put in that reservoir and, unsurprisingly, you get from it what you put in it.

It's ridiculous to assume that you will be able to dip and find patience and gentleness to deal with your children if you only pour selfishness and greed into your reservoir. You don't get beans if you plant corn, in other words.

Matthew 12:35 says, "A good man out of the good treasure of his heart brings forth good things, and an evil man out of the evil treasure brings forth evil things."

What's in your heart? Has it been washed clean by Jesus? Are you regularly spending time with the Father, becoming more like Him and growing the fruit of His Spirit? Or are you too busy with things of the world to make space for Him?

When it comes time to show agape, if we have a reservoir that's drained of God's love, we have nothing to give. If we spend all our time and energy promoting our own needs, we will have nothing left to meet someone else's needs.

And if we are unable to love other people, we are not showing God love, and we are like the goats who are destined for eternal separation from God. Yikes. That's scary, isn't it?

However, imagine if you invest your time and energy into filling that reservoir with godly things? What would your life be like if you planted holy seeds?

Seeds not for *your* harvest but for *God's kingdom* harvest. Yet we so often focus on what we can get out of serving God with agape and extending that agape to other.

The very statement, "What do I get out of it?" is an agape killer. Do we understand the promise of sowing and reaping? What honestly do we need? God says He will take care of those needs:

> "Therefore do not worry, saying, 'What shall we eat?' or 'What shall we drink?' or 'What shall we wear?' For after all these things the Gentiles seek. For your heavenly Father knows that you need all these things. But seek first the kingdom of God and His righteousness, and all these things shall be added to you.
> **—Matthew 6:31–33**

If I am living in God's kingdom, I already have access to everything I need. Honestly, if I simply focus on His kingdom first, He will meet every need according to His riches, strength, and glory. When I selfishly want to build my own kingdom, that's when I run into lack. The rich young ruler from Mark 10 could not see the offer of Jesus because of his own stuff.

Let's take it further. Our lack of faith causes us to fear

that if we live generously, people will take advantage of us and we will become a doormat. If we truly live with agape, we will be used by others. Isn't that supposedly the cry of our hearts? You know, *"Use me Lord. Use me to bring glory to Your Name!"*

If our reservoir is not being filled through relationship with Him, we will run on empty and that will lead to us feeling abused. When our reservoir is flowing from Him, we will honestly not worry about giving to others because we recognize His kingdom supply is more than enough.

When we plant supernatural seeds in faith, then agape grows naturally in our lives. Let us sow in faith—agape in others who can give us nothing in return, as if to the Lord—and watch the triangle of love increase the kingdom abilities in our life to tangibly give. This will increase the size and strength of our branch so we have more flow from the Lord and can give out more fruit.

Your children and grandchildren will be blessed by what comes from your reservoir. When difficulties strike, you have a deep well from which to draw and won't be shaken by whatever may come. When you are weary, there is cool, refreshing water to quench your tired spirit. And you will be able to pour out love on everyone around you, never running dry.

Next time your family is together for Thanksgiving and your uncle starts mouthing off again, upsetting your mom and getting everyone riled up, you can speak truth into the situation with love. You have a deep well you've been investing in, so you can be the port in the storm who blesses everyone around you. You can operate not from emotion but from the Spirit—not allowing your soul to be led by the flesh, but by the Spirit, as stated in Galatians 5.

Jesus' Example

There's an interesting parallel between Jesus and the rich young ruler. Did you ever notice that Jesus Himself is a rich young ruler? He, too, followed all the commands set out in the Old Testament. However, Jesus gave up everything in order to love us. Where the young ruler failed, Jesus succeeded.

Of course, we know that Jesus was connected to the deep reservoir of God the Father's kingdom goodness. Every single interaction Jesus had with anyone was an example of agape. He was filled with good things.

Are you investing in the good things or in the evil things in your life? What return on your investment can you expect? Will you follow Jesus' example and lay down your life for an eternal treasure? Will you choose to agape those who have rejected you and Jesus? Will you move first? Will you risking rejection to love first? He did for you. Do it to others as unto Him.

Peter, do you agape me? Go spread seed. The fruit of the Spirit has good seed—so spread it. I give to my branches so they can freely produce fruit and spread seed. The fruit of agape gives life and spreads seed.

Chapter Eleven Questions

Question: What are some things other than Christ that you depend on to fill your life with meaning and to give you a sense of identity and purpose? After reading this book, how will you change what fills your inner reservoir?

_____

_____

_____

_____

_____

_____

_____

_____

_____

_____

Question: Compare and contrast Jesus and the Rich Young Ruler. Which one are you more like? Why?

_____

_____

_____

_____

_____

_____

_____

_____

Memorize and Personalize: Memorize Matthew 12:35. Make a list of the good things with which you want your heart to be filled and how you will allow God to fill you with these qualities.

_____

_____

_____

_____

_____

_____

_____

_____

Further Study: Look back over your notes from this book. Identify three specific ways that you will begin to allow God's agape love to flow through you. Remember that this is something you can only do as you are abiding in Christ and relying on His strength.

_____

_____

_____

_____

_____

_____

_____

_____

Chapter Eleven Notes

CHAPTER TWELVE

How to Wreck a Church with Love

Before we conclude this book. I want to share the effects of agape on my life and church. Don't be afraid of this chapter title, because although it's true, it may be easily misunderstood.

The best scripture I can use to explain what I mean when I say, "How to wreck a church with love," is Luke 14:25–33, on the cost of being a disciple:

Now great multitudes went with Him. And He turned and said to them, "If anyone comes to Me and does not hate his father and mother, wife and children, brothers and sisters, yes, and his own life also, he cannot be My disciple. And whoever does not bear his cross and come after Me cannot be My disciple. For which of you, intending to build a tower, does not sit down first and count the cost, whether he has enough to finish it—lest, after he has laid the foundation, and is not able to finish, all who see it begin to mock him, saying, 'This man began to build and was not able to finish'? Or what king, going to make war against another king, does not sit down first and consider whether he is

able with ten thousand to meet him who comes against
him with twenty thousand? Or else, while the other is still
a great way off, he sends a delegation and asks conditions
of peace. So likewise, whoever of you does not forsake all
that he has cannot be My disciple.

This scripture was the text of the first message I ever
spoke. I was twelve years old when I preached for the first
time. The enemy came after me hard. I submitted to the
enemy of my soul and rebelled against God. At that time,
I was not aware of that the enemy was trying to destroy
the potential I had to glorify God. The scripture above
makes it plain that nothing should come before our obedience to Christ. Often we think that means everything is in
competition with our relationship with Christ. Nothing
could be further from the truth. When we are in unity with
Christ, everything flows from this place of divine peace.
The flow we receive from is what causes fruit. It produces
unity among the brethren. There may be persecution happening around the corner but that doesn't mean God is
going to leave you or forsake you.

A number of years ago we had a good church, a na-
tional television broadcast, and we were seeing people
saved. We were a good, working- to middle-class family
church. We had plans for and started to break ground for
a new auditorium. That's not where I started but it's where
we were headed.

I had started in ministry reaching out to youth who
were overlooked. They were the kids no one had time for,
but everyone was concerned about. We began to grow as
we simply reached out to them. Weekly ministry, youth
camps, outreaches, training and leadership discipleship

ministry. God was doing great things.

I had taken over as the head pastor at the church where I had co pastored and pioneered with my father for many years. We had a good church and solid steady growth was happening.

We went through (the best way I could put it, being sensitive to everyone involved) some very troubled waters. I honestly wanted to give up and walk away. But that wasn't the Lord's plan. We got through the troubled waters, but we had suffered some loss, personally and financially. Yet God was with us, and His visitation was evident.

God was pouring out His favor on us, but honestly, I didn't want to be just the same family church we had lulled ourselves into before. I felt like God was asking for something more, something different. To make a long church history somewhat shorter, we began to make some very incremental changes that profoundly altered our trajectory. We put a statement above our church, and it's still there today: "Value every person." It's something every church tries to do, but we knew God was compelling us to take it further. We began to actively reach out to the broken in ways we had only done from a distance for years. Now we were bringing the hurting and broken into our church in ways we had never done before.

We began to actively seek out hurting people. At first it was okay, but then it began to make some people in the congregation uncomfortable. We have always been an outreach church, mostly to youth, but now we are reaching out to everyone—and I mean everyone. I could tell you stories that most of you wouldn't even believe. The message of "win the lost at any cost" was fully on our lips. I'm not sure we would have had the courage to continue if we had known the cost beforehand.

We started talking about what it meant to agape in reality, to pour it all out to those who could give you nothing. We began to expand our feeding and clothing outreaches.

I wish I could tell you that when we stepped out in this way, the church exploded in finances and growth. But that wouldn't be the truth. God began to expand our ministry and provide for us—but not with upper-middle-class, easy-to-deal-with people. Instead, He began to trust us with the broken and hurting. For many of our steady and faithful families, it was more than they could take. I don't say that with criticism, but I did feel sad to lose people I love from my congregation. Many were very vital to our financial stability, but God has remained faithful. Our support isn't traditional, but it's of the kingdom of God, who continues to provide emotionally, spiritually, and financially. We don't always know how and when, but God is faithful to us while we are faithful to loving people.

In all honestly, I would rather serve Jesus with the courageous people we have now than with anyone else. We may not all be noble, or wise, or even beautiful (I think they are all that and more, but the world and even the religious church may not). One thing I can say about the people we labor with: they agape. When we face an earth-shattering crisis, they agape. A pandemic, they agape. Fires burning, they agape. The many or the one, they agape.

We changed the format of our church to allow for more

one-on-one time with hurting people at each campus and at each church service. It has created a church I am proud to call home. It has created a church that risks, a church that loves, and a church that is pouring out the heart of God through agape.

Based on worldly measurements of success, we are nothing as a people or as a church. We may have wrecked a good, middle-class family church. What we have now is a church that looks like the family church (bride) of Christ. He is perfecting us. We are beautiful, and we are successful, as we agape Him extravagantly by loving the least of these whom He calls the most.

To close out this chapter, let's look at Luke 14:34:

Salt is good; but if the salt has lost its flavor, how shall it be seasoned?

Salt is cohesive. It binds together, it flavors, it preserves. Let's be that kind of people. Let us be the people of God who show forth His glory by showing forth His amazing agape.

By this all will know that you are My disciples, if you have love for one another.
—John 13:35

The church has been denoted by our buildings, our power, our influence for way too long. What if the church were known for our love? For our agape? The Bible says they will know us by our love. May the whole world know us by our agape for each other and the world!

I challenge every church pastor, leader, and congregant: are we loving the outcast? Are we loving those without with our exact passion? Are we elevating the elevated or are we raising the broken-hearted and binding up their wounds? Are we the religious or are we leaving that to the good Samaritans outside of our church? We often just pass them by.

Don't get me wrong. We might let them into our church—but how do we make them feel? Do they get the same warm welcome? Are they invited to the small groups? Are we going into the highways and byways and compelling them to come in?

As the church, we are the Bride of Christ! We are the ones called out of darkness into His glorious light, that we might show forth His unconditional love, expecting nothing in return. Let us not love from a distance. Instead, let us love others right into our church and right into our homes. Let us wreck our religious institutions to look a lot more like life-saving stations—hospitals for the broken, instead of country clubs for the religious.

Let our worship be in action first before just simple songs on our lips. Let the Word of God burn in our souls and be found in the way we live and love. May the Lord revive us! Let us wreck our good churches to be found as a great, glorious habitation of God's presence once again.

WORKBOOK

Chapter Twelve Questions

Question: Have you counted the cost of what it means to be a disciple of Christ? In what ways has the cost of discipleship surprised you? How is agape a fruit of taking up your cross and following Jesus? How would you rate your love and the love of your church? Do you help from afar or do you bring others into your life?

_____

_____

_____

_____

_____

_____

_____

_____

_____

Question: Does your life reveal agape to the point where the world can look at you and see a love greater than they have known or experiences? What ways can you step out to show agape more radically?

_____

_____

_____

_____

_____

_____

_____

_____

Memorize and Personalize: Memorize Luke 14: 28–33. In what ways has God called you to forsake all for His cause? Have you responded with willingness?

_____

_____

_____

_____

_____

_____

_____

Further Study: Look up churches or ministries (whether your own or a different one) that are living agape in a unique way. What are they doing that stands out to you? What can you learn from them and how can you apply it to your life? If it's a part of your own church, how can you start participating in those ministries or outreaches? How can you teach your children to agape through living, genuine acts of service and a life of loving the unlovely?

_____

_____

_____

_____

_____

_____

_____

_____

_____

_____

Chapter Twelve Notes

CHAPTER THIRTEEN

How Could a Loving God…?

"How could a loving God…?" This is the statement most commonly made in accusation against our loving God. The God who is agape. The answer to this question is simply found following the most widely known scripture around the world. What follows John 3:16? Maybe we could answer our own questions if we simply read on in Scripture. Read on, young man or woman, read on:

For God so loved the world that He gave His only begotten Son, that whoever believes in Him should not perish but have everlasting life. For God did not send His Son into the world to condemn the world, but that the world through Him might be saved.

He who believes in Him is not condemned; but he who does not believe is condemned already, because he has not believed in the name of the only begotten Son of God. And this is the condemnation, that the light has come into the world, and men loved darkness rather than light, because their deeds were evil. For everyone practicing evil hates the light and does not come to the light, lest his deeds should be exposed. But he who does the truth comes to the

light, that his deeds may be clearly seen, that they have been done in God."
—John 3:16–21

God didn't have to come to condemn the world because it was already condemned and needed a Savior. Jesus came that we would have eternal life with Him. Eternal life is a life in Christ Jesus that begins as we confess Him as our Lord. It is a life we begin now, experiencing His outpouring of love and pouring it out into the world in which we live. That is the way people will know we are of God. When we love like Jesus did, we will see people's lives changed. If we ask, "How could a loving God…?" I want to ask, how could a people whom God has revealed His love to not love others the same way He has loved them? We can use the same fruit (the fruit of the Holy Spirit) He has given to us to pour out on others.

You may have felt unworthy of His love. You have to ask yourself, am I seeking love incorrectly? If you are, that might mean you're giving love incorrectly as well. Do you find your value in your reputation and occupation? We often feel God loves us because of what we do and who we are.

We don't love others to get God to love us, but simply because He does love us. It's an outpouring of the God's love. We show love and appreciation to God by loving others. This brings light to our daily walk and causes us to live in greater wisdom and power. We can walk in His love when we embrace His love and accept Him as our Savior and Lord. If you haven't yet begun to do that, today is the day to begin. When you begin to forgive as you are forgiven and freely love as you are freely loved, you will see a light shed in your life. When you give, it will be given to you in abundance.

> *A new commandment I give to you, that you love one another; as I have loved you, that you also love one another. By this all will know that you are My disciples, if you have love for one another.*
>
> **—John 13:34–35**

We end this book just like we started it, with Jesus asking, "Do you love (agape) Me? We can answer, "Yes." Check that "Yes" box. It is not done by our works and deeds. We don't answer this question by how much we have given in the offering or through our church attendance. We don't even answer it by the hours of worshiping at His feet. It's not that we don't do those things, but they are all secondary to simply loving others the way He loves us. Knowing His love is never-ending and will never fail us, we can dare to reach out and unconditionally love others.

We simply tend, feed and love like He does and by doing this, the world will know we belong to Jesus.

WORKBOOK

Chapter Thirteen Questions

Question: If someone asks you, "How could God condemn a world He loves?" how would you respond?

_____

_____

_____

_____

_____

_____

_____

_____

Question: How will the world be changed?

_____

_____

_____

_____

_____

_____

_____

_____

_____

Memorize and Personalize: Memorize the Great Commission. If not me, then who? If not now, then when?

_____

_____

_____

_____

_____

_____

_____

_____

_____

Chapter Thirteen Notes

CONCLUSION

Agape Transforms

When the disciples were following Jesus during His three years of ministry, they did a lot of nonsensical things. They shooed the children away from Jesus (Matthew 19:13). They argued over which of them would be the most important in the kingdom of God (Mark 10:35–45). They fell asleep when Jesus urged them to pray (Matthew 26:36–46). In short, they weren't showing agape.

There was a remarkable change between the disciples before Jesus' death and resurrection, and afterward. Once they received the Holy Spirit by becoming new creatures in Christ Jesus as an act of agape, they were forever transformed by the Holy Spirit. Ten of the remaining eleven disciples were killed for the sake of the gospel. Peter became an example of the rock of truth on which the church was built (Matthew 16:18). They were beaten, driven from towns, and imprisoned. Yet, they didn't recant or quit.

God's agape is transformative. It calls us into greater

fellowship and grafts us into His tree which allows us to produce remarkable fruit. Experiencing God's agape awakens in us a desire to change.

Like Jesus did, it may be time to pull away to the desert and pray. It's time to keep the heart of Jesus burning in you. To find the passion you had for Christ in the beginning—the kind of passion that fills you to a place of overflowing. You should overflow so much so, that when life squeezes you, love flows out to others.

Yet most people, like the rich young ruler, see the weight of the call and turn away. So many of us sit in church eating the fruit that other people have grown, while growing none or very little of our own.

I pray that you will bloom and grow tremendous agape fruit. I hope that you will draw near to God and understand the depth of His awesome love for you. In response, I hope you will begin to love all the people in your life with agape until it comes as naturally as breathing to you.

We have a world waiting for us. They are in desperate need of the fruit of the Spirit to be poured out to them. Please actively and intentionally begin to give your life away and watch the Lord continually replenish you with more than you can ever give away. I leave you with this:

> *But seek ye first the kingdom of God, and his righteousness; and all these things shall be added unto you. Take therefore no thought for the morrow: for the morrow shall take thought for the things of itself. Sufficient unto the day is the evil thereof.*
> *—Matthew 6:33–34 (KJV)*

He who is asking is faithful. He's asking you, *"Do you agape Me?"* You can joyfully respond, "Yes, Lord, I agape You." Go out and continue to feed His little ones the fruit of agape. This is how you show your love to God; this is how the world will come to know Him.

REFERENCES

Notes

1. Strong, James. "G25: *agapao*." *A Concise Dictionary of the Words in the Greek Testament and the Hebrew Bible*. Faithlife, 2019.

2. Strong, "G25: *agapao*," *A Concise Dictionary*.

3. Lexico, "eros." https://www.lexico.com/definition/eros.

4. Strong, "G5368: *phileo*," *A Concise Dictionary*.

5. Strong, "G5546: *Christianos*," *A Concise Dictionary*.

6. Strong, "G5547: *Christos*," *A Concise Dictionary*.

7. Strong, "G25: *agapao*," *A Concise Dictionary*.

8. Strong, "G5368: *phileo*," *A Concise Dictionary*.

9. Strong, "G25: *agapao*," *A Concise Dictionary*.

10. Strong, "G5368: *phileo*," *A Concise Dictionary*.

11. Strong, "G5368: *phileo*." *A Concise Dictionary*.

12. Strong, "G5368: *phileo*." *A Concise Dictionary*.

13. Strong, "G5387: *philostorgos*," *A Concise Dictionary*.

14. McDowell, Sean. *The Fate of the Apostles: Examining the Martyrdom Accounts of the Closest Followers of Jesus.* Ashgate Publishing, 2015.

About the Author

Despite being adopted into a family who loved and accepted him, Pastor Aaron Taylor has experienced his share of feeling rejected, unwanted and unloved. He used to reject the very thing God was trying hard to express to him: His unconditional love. Aaron asked many times, "Do You love me?"—until one day, an amazing revelation of God's love changed his life forever.

Aaron Taylor has six children (one who, like him, was adopted). Over the years, many have been brought into his personal home, as well as the homes provided by his church for a time of healing. He and his wife have a growing number of much-loved grandchildren.

He has pastored the same church for over thirty years (Crossfire Healing House Church in Eugene/Springfield, Oregon). His sermons have been aired on television locally and nationally and have been shared around the world. (Many are available currently at www.mycrossfire.com.)

Pastor Taylor and his wife have a passion for people and missions. Together, and as a family, they travel to many third-world countries to share the love of God in tangible and non-tangible ways. This book is the first of many in his heart.

If you would like to have Pastor Aaron share at your conference, retreat, or church, please contact him at info@mycrossfire.com or write him at:

Crossfire World Outreach Church
c/o Pastor Aaron
942 28th Street
Springfield, OR 97477

About Renown Publishing

Renown Publishing was founded with one mission in mind: to make your great idea famous.

At Renown Publishing, we don't just publish. We work hard to pair strategy with innovative marketing techniques so that your book launch is the start of something bigger.

Learn more at RenownPublishing.com.

Made in the USA
Middletown, DE
14 February 2022

60823137R00106